Horses

BY KATE REDDICK

A Ridge Press Book

Bantam Books
Toronto • New York • London

Photo Credits

AP—Animal Photography Ltd.   PR—Photo Researchers
BC—Bruce Coleman   PM—Pictor Milano
LP—Lefa Publications   RG—Rapho Guillumette
M—Mauritius

Abel (M): 77; Godfrey Argent: 81, 93; K. Barkleigh-Shute: 43, 94; J. Behnke (PM): 29 (top); Big Mike (PM): 53; E. M. Bordis (PM): 84 (top), 85; Gunnar Dahl (AP): 37 (btm.); W. Ferchland (PM): 27 (left); Kenneth W. Fink (BC): 39 (top); John S. Flannery (BC): 79; W. L. Hamilton (PM): 58; Marshall P. Hawkins: 82, 91 (btm.); A. J. Hewerdine (BC): 12 (top rt.); Institut Superieur D'Agriculture, Sofia: 101, 119; Bank Langmore: 86 (top); LBMLF, Vienna (PR): 75 (btm.); Florian J. Lem: 99, 123 (btm.), 124; D. Lohr (M): 12 (btm.); Larry L. Lowman: 89; S. Masser (PM): 11, 31; Walter D. Osborne (PR): 102; Godfrey Pasco-Wood (BC): 140-141; Photo Remy: 118; Photostore: 3, 34; Pictor Ltd.: 13, 15, 26, 37 (top); Pony of the Americas Club: 38; Porterfield-Chickering (PR): 14; Mrs. Z. Raczkowska (AP): 107; Hans Reinhard (BC): 90-91, (PM), 44; Revers-Widauer (PM): 109, 138 (top); H. Armstrong Roberts: 5, 50, 56 (btm.), 69; Peter Roberts: 25, 45 (btm.), 112 (btm.); George Rodger: 12 (top left), 20, 32, 46, 47 (top), 74, 108 (top), 116, 117, 141 (btm.); F. Rust (PM): 47 (btm.); Schmidecker (M): 41 (top); Dirk Schwager (LP): 4, 16-17, 21, 29 (btm.), 61, 97; Cliff Shelley: 28; H. Silvester (RG): 19; George Smallsreed (U.S. Trotting Assn.): 104; Tom Stack: 39 (btm.); Prof. Staun (AP): 121, 136; A. Thau (PM): 112 (top); Sally Anne Thompson (AP): 18, 23, 24, 30, 33, 35, 40, 41 (btm.), 42, 45 (top); 51, 52, 54, 55, 59, 60, 63, 64, 65, 70, 71, 72, 73, 76, 80, 83, 86 (btm.), 92, 95, 96, 98, 100, 105, 106, 108 (btm.), 110-111, 114, 115, 120, 123, 125 (btm.), 126, 128, 130, 131, 132, 134, 135, 137, 139, 142, 143, 144, 145, 146; Joe Van Wormer (BC): 78-79; Waldkirch (M): 68; F. Walther (PM): 138 (btm.); Elisabeth Weiland (RG): 27 (rt.), 36, 56 (btm.); 62, 66, 67, 75 (top), 88, 125 (top), 127, 147; Charles Perry Weimer: 48, 49; Maynard Frank Wolfe (Globe Photos): 84 (btm.)

Front Cover: Thoroughbred, Albert Squillace
Back Cover: Arab mare, Dirk Schwager (LP)
Title Page: Top, French Trotter; bottom left, Suffolk Punch;
bottom right, Arab. All, George Rodger
Drawings: Robert J. Lee

HORSES
A Bantam Book published by arrangement with The Ridge Press, Inc.
Text prepared under the direction of Dr. Alan Isaacs, Science Director,
Laurence Urdang Associates, Ltd. Designed and produced
by The Ridge Press, Inc. All rights reserved.
Copyright 1976 in all countries of the International Copyright Union
by The Ridge Press, Inc. This book may not be reproduced
in whole or in part by mimeograph or any other means, without permission.
For information address: The Ridge Press, Inc.,
25 West 43rd Street, New York, N.Y. 10036.
Library of Congress Catalog Card Number: 75-21601
D.L. TO-958-80
ISBN 0-553-14875-3
Published simultaneously in the United States and Canada.

Bantam Books are published by Bantam Books, Inc.
Its trademark, consisting of the words "Bantam Books" and the portrayal
of a bantam, is registered in the United States Patent Office
and in other countries. Marca Registrada.
Bantam Books, Inc., 666 Fifth Avenue, New York, N.Y. 10019.
Printed in Spain by Artes Gráficas Toledo, S.A.
11 10 9 8 7 6

Contents

Anglo-Arab

Carthusian ▶
▼ Nonius

Thoroughbreds

Introduction

Evolution of the Horse

The story of the modern horse, *Equus caballus,* began in the Lower Eocene period, about 60 million years ago. The earliest horse, eohippus or "dawn horse," was no more than 10 to 20 inches in height and probably lived in forests. It had broad, padded feet with four toes on the forefeet and three on the hind, each terminating in a tiny hoof. Its simple, low-crowned teeth were suited for browsing on leaves, and its eye sockets were lower on the head than in the modern horse.

The first fossil remains of this small creature were discovered at Stud Hill in Kent, England, in 1839. Not at first recognized as a member of the horse family (Equidae), it was named *Hyracotherium* (hyrax beast), which is still the correct scientific name. Somewhat older and more complete fossils were subsequently discovered in the southern United States, where it is believed the horse family originated. Eohippus spread throughout North America and eventually migrated to western Europe across the land bridge at the Bering Strait. In Europe and Asia there was great diversification: some of the descendants of eohippus became so distinct that they are not now regarded as horses. By the end of the Lower Eocene all these different lines had become extinct.

Meanwhile, in North America, changes of a much more gradual, less divergent nature were taking place. Except for the teeth, which became increasingly adapted for a diet of soft, leafy herbage, there is little to distinguish *Hyracotherium* from the two successive Eocene genera, *Orohippus* and *Epihippus.* These changes in tooth structure progressed still further through the next two stages, *Mesohippus* and *Miohippus,* and by the end of the Oligocene the dentition of horses had reached almost maximum efficiency for browsing on soft vegetation. The feet, too, had become modified. The fourth toe of the forefeet had disappeared and the lateral toes were becoming much slighter, so that most of the weight of the body was borne on the middle toes. Fossils of both *Mesohippus* and *Miohippus* indicate a definite if irregular trend toward an increase in average size.

During the next geological period, the Miocene, the horse family split into numerous collateral branches. Some of the groups continued as forest browsers. Of these animals, some remained small, while others, notably *Megahippus,* showed a dramatic increase in size; at least two groups reached Asia and Europe: *Anchitherium* and, later, *Hyohippus.* As changes occurred in the climate and vegetation of both

North America and Eurasia, however, these browsing horses gradually became extinct; none survived the Lower Pliocene.

The replacement of forests by grasslands over much of North America during the Miocene resulted in the emergence of a completely new type of horse—the grazer. This change in type is first seen in *Parahippus* but is more clearly marked in the later *Merychippus*. Grazing horses adapted so successfully to the plains that by the end of the Miocene at least six distinct groups were distributed over the spreading prairies of North America. These horses developed a complex dentition, similar to that of the modern horse, capable of dealing with tough, abrasive herbage; their feet, too, had evolved to suit the firmer ground. The central toe had become greatly enlarged, carrying almost the entire body weight; the lateral toes had become much smaller.

One of these prairie horses, *Hipparion,* migrated to Asia via the land bridge at the Bering Strait. During the Pliocene it spread rapidly into Europe and finally reached Africa, becoming probably the first horse to appear on that continent. *Hipparion* itself became extinct in both the Old and New Worlds in the Lower Miocene.

Back in North America the final major step in the evolution of the horse had taken place with the appearance of *Pliohippus*—the first single-toed member of the family. With the lateral toes now reduced to mere vestiges, these animals, like the modern horse, moved on the single hoof of each foot. Other anatomical and physiological changes brought their overall appearance very close to that of the horse today. One branch of this stock migrated to South America.

At the end of the Pliocene, about a million years ago, *Equus* itself arose from *Pliohippus* and quickly spread over North and South America, Europe, and Asia. About 10,000 years ago *Equus* became extinct in North America and shortly afterward disappeared from South America; it was later reintroduced by man from Europe. Thus, the only horses to survive into modern times were the descendants of those animals that had migrated to the Old World before the rising waters of the post-Glacial period.

Development of Types and Breeds

The earliest modern representatives of the horse family were divided into four main groups: the horse in Europe and Asia; the wild ass in north

Type 1

Type 3

Type 2

Type 4

Africa; the Asiatic wild ass (onager); and the zebra in southeast Africa.

Opinions as to how exactly the horse developed from this point vary greatly, but there are two main schools of thought. Some authorities believe that all modern breeds are descended from a single type of wild horse, closely resembling, if not actually identical to, Przewalski's horse. The other school postulates that even before the horse was domesticated there existed at least two, some say as many as six, distinct primitive races. The proponents of this theory maintain that the great range of size and the variety of color and form found within the species today could not have resulted from human intervention alone. A most recent theory supporting this view distinguishes four separate types:

Type 1—a type of pony inhabiting northwestern Europe. Standing about 12.2 hands and bay or brown in color, it had a straight facial profile, broad forehead, small ears, wide nostrils, and a thick mane and tail. It was very similar to the Exmoor pony of today.

Type 2—a type of pony, the most northerly and most widely distributed group, inhabiting northern Eurasia. Reaching a height of 14.2 hands, it had a full tail and stiff, erect mane, but little or no fetlock. Altogether more heavily built than Type 1, with a coarser head and larger ears, it was slightly convex in profile and closely resembled Przewalski's horse.

Type 3—a type of horse inhabiting central Asia. Standing up to 15 hands, and distinctly convex in profile, it had a sparse mane and tail, long, narrow head, long ears, a long, straight neck, flat sides, and a sloping croup.

Type 4—a type of horse inhabiting western Asia. Standing at about 12 hands, narrow and fine-boned, it had small ears, a short head, short back, flat croup, fine coat, and an abundant, silky mane and high-set tail. It was concave in profile and broad between the eyes. This type is resembled by the recently discovered Caspian pony of Iran.

The extent to which each of these four types would have been capable of increasing in size if no crossbreeding had taken place would have varied considerably. Under favorable climatic and feeding conditions Types 3 and 4 would have grown bigger. Type 2 had the greatest potential, limited only by the amount of food available and by the amount of protection it could find against the cold and damp.

Some crossbreeding of the four types is thought to have taken place

Haflinger ponies

in the wild state. Although natural barriers kept the different groups apart, their territories overlapped extensively and some mingling must have occurred in the overlap zones. This would have resulted in an increase in size. As man gradually domesticated the horse, further crossing of the four types is believed to have taken place.

At first this would have been in a very haphazard manner, especially as the horse in the early stages of domestication was probably used simply as a source of meat and milk. The most frequent cross with Type 1 would have been Type 2, its nearest neighbor; it is thought that most of the north European native ponies have blood of these two types in varying proportions. When Type 2 was crossed with Type 3 and fed and sheltered in the winter, a taller and heavier animal would have been produced—the forerunner of the medieval warhorse and the modern European draft breeds. The cross between Types 3 and 4, sheltered from the heat during the dry season, would again have led to an increase in stature; the modern light horse breeds are believed to be derived basically from crosses of these two types.

As man began to use the horse increasingly for other purposes, more selective crosses were made to obtain the specialized types required. This process led eventually to the emergence of the breeds known today. Although the three basic groups of domesticated horses (pony, light horse, and heavy horse) derived from the primitive races have remained the same, the pattern within each group has changed constantly and continues to change in response to new demands.

Editor's Note: Only after considerable research and difficulties were we able to obtain a photograph of the Russian Novokirghiz. Although not available in color, this photo has nevertheless been included so you may see this interesting animal.

Ponies

American Shetland

As a result of careful selective breeding, the American Shetland pony has evolved into a much more refined and elegant type than its British counterpart. It tends to be somewhat taller (the average height is about 42 inches) and the height limit, 46 inches, is greater than that of the Island type (42 inches).

In common with the parent breed, the American Shetland may be of any color. It also has the same profuse mane and tail, but its coat is much finer and sleeker. The head is small and elegant, often with a slightly dished profile reminiscent of the Arab and other eastern breeds; the body is compact and well muscled, with comparatively long, fine legs.

In spite of its rather delicate appearance, the American Shetland is extremely hardy and robust; it is used and shown both under saddle and in harness.

14   Compare **Shetland** (p. 41).

Preceding pages, left to right:
(top) Welsh, Haflinger, New Forest;
(btm.) Shetland, Avelignese.

Avelignese

A typical mountain breed, the Avelignese is found throughout the mountainous areas of northern, central, and southern Italy, especially in the Trentino-Alto Adige and Veneto regions of the northeast. It is related to the Haflinger of Austria, having descended from a common ancestor, the old Avellinum-Haflinger, and the two breeds show marked similarities in coloration and conformation.

Standing 13.3 to 14.2 hands in height, the Avelignese is chestnut, often with white markings, and has a full, light or flaxen mane and tail. Tough and muscular in its general appearance, it has a short, rather heavy neck, powerful quarters, short sturdy legs, and hard joints and hoofs.

The breed, noted for its longevity and docile temperament, is used mainly for pack transport in the mountains and for light agricultural work.

Basuto

In 1653 Arabs and Barbs from Java were brought to the Cape region of southern Africa by the Dutch East India Company. These were the first horses to arrive in southern Africa, an area without indigenous horses, and they formed the foundation of the Cape horse. Until the end of the seventeenth century the breed continued to be reinforced by fresh imports of oriental stock and, especially from 1770 to 1790, by Thoroughbreds brought from England. From the early nineteenth century onward, Cape horses began to arrive in Basutoland (now Lesotho), where they evolved into the type known as the Basuto pony.

Standing about 14.2 hands, the Basuto is normally chestnut, bay, brown, or gray. It is a thickset animal, with a fairly long back, short legs, and extremely hard hoofs, and is noted for sure-footedness, courage, and exceptional stamina.

Viatka

Said to be based on the Klepper, a type of light draft horse found in Estonia, the Viatka is bred in the northwest of the Soviet Union. Here it is used mainly in harness for light farm work and transport, especially in troikas.

It stands 13 to 14 hands and is a hardy, frugal animal with a lively, willing temperament. It has a longish, slightly dished face, a deep, broad chest, fairly long, straight back, and well-sprung ribs. The legs are short and hard, with about 7 inches of bone below the knee, but the hind legs tend to be narrowly set on and sickle-hocked. The usual colors are dun, gray, or roan, and many Viatkas have a dark dorsal stripe and dark zebra stripes under the shoulders. The breed is noted for its peculiar short, but very fast, trotting gait, which is particularly effective over snow.

Camargue

A very ancient breed, thought by some to be descended from the prehistoric Solutré horse with later infusions of Barb and Arab blood, the Camargue lives in semi-wild herds inhabiting the marshlands of the Rhône delta in southeastern France. The rough terrain, sparse pasture, and severe climate have produced a remarkably hardy, sure-footed animal, used traditionally by the *gardians* (the local cowboys) for herding bulls.

Standing between 13.1 and 14.2 hands, the Camargue has a rough, invariably gray coat, a square head with a straight or concave profile and wide-set eyes, short, thick neck, a large barrel, often with a goose rump, and short, sturdy legs.

The breed was accorded official recognition as recently as 1967, and, under the auspices of the State Stud Administration, a breeders' association has now been formed.

Caspian

The existence of the Caspian was discovered as recently as 1965, when a few specimens were found roaming wild on the shores of the Caspian Sea in northern Iran. It is thought that these small horses, estimated at about 50, are the direct descendants of Iran's prehistoric wild horse, a miniature horse used by the Mesopotamians in the third millennium B.C. and believed to have died out over 1,000 years ago.

A strong, hardy animal of equable temperament, the Caspian stands 9.2 to 11.2 hands and is bay, chestnut, or gray, with a profuse mane and tail. It has a small, fine head with large, wide-set eyes and a narrow muzzle, an arched neck, high withers, and a narrow body with a short back and sloping croup. The legs are slender, with dense, hard bone and small, oval hoofs. The breed is very reminiscent of the Arab, of which it is claimed to have been the forerunner.

Connemara

Native to the remote uplands of the west of Connacht, in Ireland, this ancient breed is believed to have descended from primitive native ponies crossed with Spanish and, later, Arab stock. It is a hardy, sure-footed, and docile creature, which for many years has been used, especially by small farmers, as a general utility pony. Today it is valued increasingly as a child's pony, and in order to improve it for riding purposes the breed society has carried out breeding experiments using part-Arab and small Thoroughbred stallions.

Standing 13 to 14.2 hands, the Connemara is commonly gray, black, bay, brown, or dun, although roans and chestnuts are also found. It has a neat head, well-sloped shoulders, a deep, compact body, and fairly short legs with hard, flat bone measuring 7 to 8 inches below the knee. It should have a good, free action at all paces.

Most of the Connemaras bred in Ireland are still kept under natural conditions and seem to remain truer to type on poor, rough pasture than if they are stable-fed.

Dales

The Dales pony from northeastern England resembles the Fell pony of the northwest, and the two breeds almost certainly descended from a common root stock, although the Dales is larger and stockier.

For many centuries the Dales pony played an important part in the life and economy of the northeast. Hardy, strong, and, above all, adaptable, it was put to all kinds of farm work and used as a tradesman's pony, pit pony, and pack animal. With the introduction of motorized transport and machinery, the Dales pony gradually became redundant and the breed declined. However, the growing interest in pony trekking has created a demand for quiet, sensible mounts of this kind, and its numbers are now increasing.

Standing up to 14.2 hands, the Dales pony is black, bay, brown, or gray, with a compact, muscular appearance. It has strong legs with plenty of bone, hard open hoofs of a bluish color, a profuse mane and tail, and silky-feathered heels.

Dartmoor

One of nine breeds of pony native to Britain, the Dartmoor is found in the extreme southwest of England. Until a stud book was opened in 1899, Dartmoor ponies were not registered, and infusions of outside blood produced considerable variations in type. Since the formation of the breed society, efforts have been made to stabilize and standardize the breed, in spite of severe setbacks suffered during World War II, when Dartmoor became a battle training ground.

A hardy, sure-footed, compact animal not exceeding 12.2 hands, the Dartmoor has a small head with tiny ears, strong back, well-muscled loins and quarters, tough, well-shaped feet, and a full mane and tail. Although bay, brown, and black are preferred, many colors are found within the breed and only piebalds and skewbalds are barred from the stud book.

Because of its kindly, sensible nature, the Dartmoor makes an ideal first pony and, like the neighboring Exmoor, is favored by breeders as foundation stock for producing larger riding ponies.

▲ Dales ▼ Dartmoor

Exmoor

The oldest of the native British breeds, the Exmoor takes its name from the expanse of wild moorland in southwestern England that has been its home since prehistoric times. The effect of this bleak, exposed habitat has been to produce a strong, agile, and sure-footed pony, noted above all for its hardiness—a characteristic that has led to its use in many countries as foundation stock for breeding.

Not exceeding 12.2 hands (mares) or 12.3 hands (stallions), the Exmoor is bay, brown, or dun, with characteristic mealy patches on the muzzle, around the eyes, on the belly, and inside the thighs. It bears no white markings at all. In winter the coat becomes dull and thick, with a distinctive wiry texture that is peculiar to the breed. Broad and deep in the chest, with the shoulders set well back, the Exmoor has powerful loins, clean legs, small, hard feet, and a neat head with short, pointed **24** ears, broad forehead, and large, prominent eyes.

Falabella

Reputedly the smallest breed of pony in the world, the Falabella was developed in the Argentine by the Falabella family of the Recreo de Roca ranch, near Buenos Aires. It was their aim to produce a very small pony with good conformation and a good disposition. Shetland ponies were used as the foundation of the breed, and by a careful process of inbreeding, using at each mating only the smallest animals available, the height was gradually reduced to its present standard (not exceeding 30 inches at maturity). The Falabella has a fine, silky coat and all colors are found within the breed, Appaloosa markings (see p. 57) being particularly sought after.

The breed has proved very successful in various parts of the world, particularly North America, where it has become popular not only as a child's "first" pony, but also as a harness pony.

Fell

Native to Cumberland and Westmorland, in northwestern England, the
Fell pony is a strong, active, willing, and very versatile animal; it was
used in the past for a great variety of work, both in harness and under
saddle. Like the related Dales pony, it became invaluable during the
seventeenth and eighteenth centuries as a pack pony for carrying lead
from local mines to ports on the east coast.

In some parts of the Lake District it is still ridden by shepherds but
today it is valued principally as a pleasure horse and as breeding stock.
Because of the purity of the breed, it is favored as a foundation for
breeding hunters and jumpers and in many countries is used as an
improver, especially where substance is required.

Black predominates, with brown, bay, or gray also occurring. The
Fell has a flowing mane and tail and finely feathered heels; it should not
exceed 14 hands. It has a high head carriage, a broad, well-muscled
body, hard feet, and exceptionally strong legs with at least 8 inches of
26 bone below the knee.

Fjord

The Fjord pony, also called the Fjording or Westland, has a distinctly primitive appearance and is undoubtedly of very ancient origin. Standing 13 to 14.2 hands, it is a square, compact, very muscular animal with a small, neat head, often slightly concave in profile, a thick, powerful neck, and short, hard legs. It is invariably dun, with a silvery mane and tail and a black dorsal stripe, which extends from the forelock, through the mane, to the tip of the tail. Its stiff, rather coarse mane is traditionally trimmed to stand in a characteristic upright crest.

The breed is widely distributed throughout Scandinavia and has been exported in considerable numbers to Denmark, Germany, and other north European countries. Sturdy and active, the Fjord pony is still used for many kinds of agricultural work, especially in inaccessible hilly districts; it is also used for pleasure, both under saddle and in harness.

Galiceño

It is believed that the ancestors of the Galiceño originated in Galicia, in northwestern Spain, and were among the horses landed in Mexico by Cortés.

In 1959 the breed, which for centuries has been used in Mexico for transport, pack, and general ranch work, was introduced into the United States. Since then it has rapidly become established throughout the country.

In spite of its size—12 to 13.2 hands at maturity—the Galiceño is generally classed as a horse because of its general make-up and its natural, fast, running walk. Usually bay, black, sorrel, or dun (piebalds, skewbalds, and albinos are not eligible for entry in the registry), it has a fine, compact appearance and is noted for its intelligence and gentle, amenable disposition. These characteristics, combined with its stamina, courage, and versatility, make the Galiceño an excellent competition horse as well as an ideal ranch horse or family mount.

Iceland

The Iceland pony is descended from stock of Norwegian, Scottish, and, to a lesser extent, Irish origin introduced by early Norse settlers, principally during the ninth and tenth centuries. For many years these ponies were the only means of transport on the island and were used under saddle, in harness, and as pack animals. They also provided an important source of meat, especially in winter. Today some Iceland ponies are bred for draft purposes; most, however, are broken for riding and have a distinctive ambling gait known as the *tølt*.

Standing about 12 to 13 hands, these compact, sturdy, sure-footed animals are usually gray or dun. Iceland ponies are noted for their docile but independent nature and pronounced homing instinct. They are economical feeders and are extremely hardy, living mainly in semi-wild herds that remain in the open all the year round.

Hackney

The Hackney pony is in effect a smaller version of the Hackney horse (see p. 113). Its development as a distinct and separate type—virtually a separate breed, although both share the same stud book—dates from the 1880s. Christopher Wilson, a breeder from Westmorland, England, carried out a program of selective breeding using as the foundation a small Yorkshire-bred Hackney stallion called Sir George.

In spite of its close association with the Hackney horse, the Hackney pony is a true pony type. It stands 12 to 14 hands and is usually brown, bay, black, or (rarely) chestnut. It has a high head and tail carriage, a compact body with good shoulders and quarters, and strong, hard limbs with well-defined tendons. Like the Hackney horse, it is now bred almost exclusively for the show ring, where the demand is for animals with a spectacular, fluid, high-stepping action.

Haflinger

A hardy mountain pony of ancient lineage, the Haflinger is native to the South Tyrol. It is now bred principally in Austria and Germany and is also established in a number of other countries, including Britain.

Frugal, agile, and extremely strong for its size (about 13.3 hands), the Haflinger is used mainly for pack and light draft work in agriculture and forestry. Like the closely related Avelignese, it is usually chestnut, with a full flaxen mane and tail. It has a fairly long head with large eyes and small ears, a long, broad back, strong loins and quarters, and short legs with hard joints and hoofs.

During the last twenty years or so, the breed has been greatly improved in Austria as a result of strict controls imposed by the government to ensure that only the best stock is used for breeding. Like the stallions, which are all government-owned, the mares are carefully selected and must undergo a series of rigorous inspections before they can be entered in the stud book and used for breeding. **31**

Highland

Although there is only one register, it is generally accepted that there are two distinct types of Highland pony: the mainland type, which stands about 14.2 hands; and the smaller, finer Western Isles variety, between 12.2 and 13.2 hands. The latter is regarded as the pure and older strain, though at various times both types have had considerable infusions of foreign blood, notably Arabian.

A strong, sure-footed, and docile animal of true pony character, the Highland is wide between the eyes and has a neat, attractive head, deep, muscular body, and short, strong legs with plenty of bone (9 to 10 inches in stallions; 8 to 8½ inches in mares) and a tuft of hair at the fetlock. Usually black, brown, or gray, often with a dark dorsal stripe, it has a flowing mane and full but well-carried tail.

The Highland, traditionally associated with the small farmer, is still found mainly in its native Scotland, where it is used as a general utility pony.

Hucul

Native to the Carpathian Mountains in eastern Europe, the Hucul, or Huzul, is a strong, hardy pony believed to have descended directly from the tarpan, but with considerable infusions of Arab blood, according to some authorities. It is closely related to the Konik, and the two breeds show marked similarities in appearance. The Hucul, however, is somewhat smaller, usually standing between 12.1 and 13.1 hands.

A frugal, very docile and willing creature, it possesses great stamina and is used on highland farms in the Carpathians for draft work. It is also used for pack transport and the larger animals are sometimes ridden. The predominant colors are dun and bay, but piebalds are not uncommon. Like the Konik, the Hucul has a tendency to be sickle-hocked but otherwise has fairly good conformation. It has a medium-sized head, carried on a short, strong neck, a sturdy well-muscled body, and sloping quarters. The principal stud is at Siary, near Gorlice, in southern Poland.

Mérens

An ancient breed, possibly of oriental origin, the Mérens inhabits the mountains and high valleys bordering the Ariège River in the south of France. The animals live in semi-wild herds and are used locally for pack transport and light draft work. A stud book was opened in 1948.

Standing about 13.3 hands, these ponies are robust, compact, and very sure-footed, with a fairly large head, deep, broad chest, strong loins and quarters, and sturdy limbs. They have thick, hairy, black coats.

Sorraia

The primitive Sorraia inhabits the plains that lie to the north of Lisbon and extend along the Sorraia River and its tributaries into western Spain. This frugal, extremely hardy pony has managed to thrive under extreme climatic conditions and on the very poorest of keep, but the lack of good pasture has left its mark in the generally poor conformation of the breed.

Standing 12 to 13 hands, the Sorraia has a long head with a straight or slightly convex profile, a thin neck, fairly deep body with rather poor shoulders, and a straight back. It is inclined to be ewe-necked. The predominant color is dun, but creams and grays are also found. Many Sorraias have a dark dorsal stripe and some also have zebra stripes on the legs.

For centuries the Sorraia was used locally for herding cattle and for light farm work, but its numbers are now dwindling. An attempt to preserve the breed has been made by the de Andrade family, who keep a small, purebred herd.

New Forest

Native to the New Forest, an area of woodland and open heath in Hampshire, England, the New Forest pony is a somewhat mixed breed of ancient origin.

Over the centuries, stock of various other breeds was released in the forest, and from the 1890s onward attempts were made to "improve" the breed by introducing not only other native pony breeds but also such alien strains as Arab and Hackney. Until 1938, when the present breed society was formed, experiments of this kind continued. As a result, there are still variations within the breed, although a more fixed type is slowly emerging.

Of any color except piebald or skewbald, the New Forest pony stands 12 to 14.2 hands. The smaller ponies are comparatively fine, while the larger ones are altogether sturdier. Quiet, willing, easy to break, and quick to learn, the "Forester" makes an ideal child's riding pony, and the larger types are capable of carrying adults.

Northlands

For centuries the Northlands, a hardy, frugal pony of ancient origin, has been used in Norway for riding and light draft work. Until about 60 years ago, it was traditionally bred, mostly by farmers, in an apparently arbitrary fashion. After World War I a number of enthusiasts attempted to standardize and preserve the old breed and stimulate wider interest in it. In spite of this, the number of registered ponies had dwindled by 1945 to only 43, but renewed efforts since then have revitalized interest in the breed, and its numbers are again increasing.

Usually dark in color, the Northlands stands about 13 hands. It has a full mane and tail, a small, neat head with wide-set eyes, fairly short, muscular neck, a strong body with sloping shoulders and firm quarters, and extremely hard limbs.

Above and left, New Forest ▼ Northlands

Pony of the Americas

In 1956 Leslie Boomhower of Mason City, Iowa, crossed a Shetland pony with an Appaloosa mare. The outcome, Black Hand—virtually a miniature Appaloosa—proved very popular in the show ring. A stud book and registry were soon opened and a new breed, the Pony of the Americas, was established, with Black Hand as its foundation sire. There are now over 12,500 registered ponies of this breed, used entirely for show and pleasure.

To qualify for registry, a pony must be 11.2 to 13 hands at maturity and must bear true Appaloosa markings: small, circular or elliptical spots on the coat, especially concentrated over the quarters, white circling around the eyes, mottled, mud-colored skin, particularly noticeable around the muzzle, and vertically striped hoofs. The Pony of the Americas is characterized by a neat head with a dished face and large, prominent eyes, a slightly arched neck, and a full-ribbed, well-muscled body. See also **Appaloosa** (p. 57).

Przewalski's Horse

This ancient, primitive horse, *Equus przewalskii,* is believed by many authorities to be the only species of wild horse still in existence. It was discovered in Mongolia in 1881 by the Russian explorer, Colonel N. M. Przewalski.

Standing at 12 to 14 hands, Przewalski's horse is dun, with a dark-brown or black dorsal stripe and sometimes also with faint leg stripes. It has a short, erect mane and a tufted tail. Relative to its size, it has a very large head, with small eyes and ears, heavy jaws, and a mealy muzzle. The neck is short and heavy; the body is stocky with straight shoulders; and the legs are clean, short, and sturdy.

In 1902 a number of specimens were acquired by Carl Hagenbeck for his zoo in Hamburg, and there are now some 200 Asiatic wild horses in zoos throughout the world. Any purebred specimens still existing in the wild state are confined to the plains of the Altai Mountain region, in west Mongolia.

Russ

Native to the Baltic island of Gotland, off the southeastern coast of Sweden, the hardy Russ, also called the Gotland or Skogruss, is an ancient and relatively pure breed. It is thought to have descended from the tarpan with admixtures of Arab and other oriental blood. It is now bred both on the island and on the Swedish mainland, and a semi-wild herd still inhabits the island forest of Löjsta.

Commonly bay or black, although all standard colors are found within the breed, the Russ is usually 12 to 12.2 hands. It has a slightly heavy head, short, muscular neck, long back, sloping quarters, and hard legs and feet.

Although it can be rather stubborn, the Russ is generally a kindly, docile animal and is favored as a child's riding pony because of its outstanding jumping ability. It also has a very good action at the trot and **40** is used for harness racing.

Shetland

No more than 42 inches high at maturity, the Shetland—a native of the isles of Orkney and Shetland—is the smallest of the British breeds and also the strongest in relation to its size. Its origins are uncertain. Some authorities believe it was introduced by immigrants from the Biscayan coasts of France and Spain; others that it evolved from larger animals of tundra origin that migrated to the British Isles before the retreat of the ice.

Formerly used on the islands as a dual-purpose saddle and pack animal and on the mainland as a pit pony, the Shetland today is kept mainly as a pet or child's pony, though it is not always the most tractable of mounts. It is characterized by a well-shaped head with a broad forehead, sloping shoulders, a deep, thickset body, and strong, short legs. It has a profuse mane and tail, and the coat, which may be of any color, becomes extremely thick in winter.

Compare **American Shetland** (p. 14).

Konik

Like the related Hucul, the Konik is thought to be a direct descendant of the tarpan, the European wild horse. The breed is found throughout Poland and has also been introduced into other east European countries; it is of great value to the small farmer, being a docile, willing worker and an economical feeder. It is also bred on systematic lines at a number of state studs.

The Konik is a robust animal, noted for its fertility and longevity. It stands about 13 hands and is usually dun, especially blue-dun, or gray, with a profuse mane and tail. Compact and well proportioned, it has generally good conformation but is inclined to be sickle-hocked.

In the past, the Konik has been highly valued as breeding stock and has been used in the foundation of a number of Polish and Soviet breeds.

Timor

Native to the island of Timor, in Indonesia, this pony is also found in Australia and New Zealand, where it has been used for crossing with native British and other pony breeds. The Timor is used in harness and, in spite of its diminutive size (about 9 hands), also under saddle; its remarkable agility and sensible, docile disposition make it well suited for stock work. It is a willing worker—hardy, sure-footed, and strong for its size.

The Timor's large, straight-profiled head is carried on a short, thick neck. It has a deep body with a strong back and short legs with small, hard hoofs. Black, bay, and other dark colors predominate, but the breed appears to include specimens of almost every color and color pattern. **43**

Welsh Mountain

Generally regarded as the most beautiful of the British pony breeds, the Welsh Mountain pony is believed to have descended directly from primitive native stock, with some infusions of Arab, and probably also of Thoroughbred blood.

A courageous, kindly, sure-footed animal, standing no more than 12 hands, it has a graceful neck set on deep, sloping shoulders, a short, strong back, short limbs with dense, flat bone, and small, hard feet. Its head, slightly concave in profile, is neat and attractive, with small, prick ears and large, wide-set eyes. At all paces the Welsh Mountain pony has a good, free action. It is equally suitable for riding or driving and in Britain, particularly, it is favored as foundation stock for breeding children's hunters and show ponies.

Although there are numerous studs, many Mountain ponies still live in semi-wild herds in the Welsh hills. In these, the quality, hardiness, and stamina associated with the breed are particularly apparent.

Welsh

Developed largely from the Welsh Mountain pony, the Welsh pony has inherited many of its characteristics. The requirements of the stud book, however, are more specifically for a child's riding pony, with special emphasis on quality, substance, and bone. As a result, the Welsh pony is in effect a larger and stronger version of the Mountain pony. It stands up to 13.2 hands and, in common with all other Welsh strains, may be of any color except piebald or skewbald.

The Welsh pony of cob type similarly does not exceed 13.2 hands, but is altogether more stoutly built. It is a robust, active animal, with a quality head, compact, muscular body, and hard limbs. It is used in harness and is becoming increasingly popular for pony trekking.

▲ Welsh Mountain; below and left, Welsh

Light Horses

Llanero

Like many South American breeds, the Llanero of Venezuela is descended from stock principally of Spanish origin. However, it is smaller and lighter than most South American horses and has finer limbs, which may be due to the exceptionally hard conditions in Venezuela.

Purebred Llaneros normally stand between 13.2 and 14 hands and rarely exceed 14.2 hands. They have a broad, flat face, short, muscular, arched neck, a compact round-ribbed body, and strong, slender limbs with small, well-made hoofs.

Llaneros are very tough animals, noted for their great stamina, powers of endurance, and lively gaits. They make excellent cow-ponies and are widely used for this purpose. Attempts to breed a larger type of Llanero for use as an army remount have so far been unsuccessful, as any increase in size is accompanied by a loss of stamina.

Preceding pages, left to right: (top)
Hunter, French Thoroughbreds; (btm.)
Arab, Palomino, German Trotter.

Peruvian Stepping Horse

This breed, also known as the Peruvian Paso, is one of a number of closely related Latin American breeds that are distinguished by their natural, high-stepping, four-beat lateral gait—the *paso*.

Almost every color occurs within the breed, although bay, chestnut, black, and gray are the most common; height varies between 13 and 15.2 hands. Over a period of about 300 years, the combined effects of natural selection and careful breeding have produced a tough, sturdy, yet elegant animal, noted for its stamina, ability to thrive on poor keep, and kindly, amenable temperament. In relation to their size, all Pasos have an enormous heart and lungs; their legs, although fine, are extremely strong, with long, sloping pasterns and hard hoofs.

In the United States the various separate strains, under the name Paso Fino, are now being blended together to produce the ideal mount of their kind.

Albino

Albinism—the congenital absence of pigmentation from the skin and other tissues—occurs in many species of birds and animals. For this reason the Albino horse, fostered in the United States since 1937 by the American Albino Horse Club, is generally regarded as a color type or mutation rather than as a breed. However, Albinos can be said to breed true in that they often produce offspring of like coloration.

Albinos are characterized by a pinky skin, pure-white hair from birth, and translucent blue eyes. Because of the lack of pigmentation, they are prone to certain weaknesses: their skin is particularly sensitive to sunlight and their sight tends to be impaired or defective. Experiments in the United States to produce white horses with normal, healthy dark-brown eyes and less sensitive skin have already met with some success.

Alter-Real

The development of this breed began in 1747, when a stud with 300 Spanish Andalusian mares was founded in Portugal by the House of Braganza. For almost 100 years the stud flourished, supplying horses for haute école to the royal menège in Lisbon, but during subsequent political upheavals, the breeding stock was severely depleted and then almost destroyed by outcrosses with Arab and other alien strains. Eventually the breed was reestablished using Andalusian stock from the Zapata stud in Spain. Further improvements were effected after 1932 when the Ministry of the Economy took over the stud, keeping only the best of the stock for breeding.

Today the Alter is an elegant, quality saddlehorse with a naturally high, showy action, which makes it particularly suitable for haute école. Bay, chestnut, or piebald, it stands 15 to 15.2 hands. It has a small, straight head, short, arched neck, close-coupled body with a deep, broad chest and muscular croup, and hard legs with large, flat knees and strong hocks. **51**

American Saddlehorse

The American Saddlehorse, or Saddlebred, was originally developed by early settlers in Kentucky as a general utility animal under saddle and in harness.

An elegant horse with a proud head carriage, it stands 15.2 to 16.2 hands and is chestnut, bay, black, or gray. It has a fine head with prominent, wide-set eyes, a long, arched neck, compact body with powerful shoulders, a level croup and rounded quarters, and long, fine legs with well-defined tendons.

Bred today as show horses, Saddlebreds are renowned for their brilliant animated action. Depending on their training, they are known as three- or five-gaited horses. The three-gaited Saddler performs at the walk, trot, and canter and is distinguished by its roached mane and tail, the latter normally being set to produce an artificially high carriage. The five-gaited Saddler, with its flowing mane and full, high-set tail, has two additional gaits, the slow gait and the rack.

Saddlebreds are also seen in fine harness and equitation classes and are used as pleasure horses for trail riding and similar activities.

Andalusian

It is believed that horses of African and eastern origin, brought into Spain during the Moorish occupation, provided the foundation for this breed. The Andalusian, or Carthusian, was fostered and developed during the fifteenth century at the Carthusian monasteries of Jerez de la Frontera, Seville, and Cazello; it is now bred mainly at private studs in southern Spain.

A strong, handsome animal, 15.3 to 16.3 hands, the Andalusian is normally gray, more rarely bay or black, with a luxuriant silky mane and tail. It has a straight head with large eyes and a broad forehead, a longish, shapely neck, long, sloping shoulders, a round-ribbed body with a broad chest, rounded croup and broad, muscular quarters, and strong, clean-cut legs. It is noted for its kindly, docile temperament and for its naturally high-stepping action. Andalusians today are highly prized as parade horses; they are sometimes also used in bullfighting. In the past they were widely used as improvers and formed the foundation stock for a number of breeds, including the Alter-Real.

53

Anglo-Arab (English)

A composite breed—a mixture of Arab and Thoroughbred—the Anglo-Arab is found in a number of countries but is most closely associated with France and Britain. In Britain the Anglo-Arab is defined as a horse whose pedigree contains no strain of blood other than Arab and Thoroughbred. The registry, administered by the Arab Horse Society, admits home-bred animals only if their ancestry on the Arab side is registered in the Arab Horse Stud Book, or in the Arab section of the General Stud Book, and if their Thoroughbred ancestry is entered in the General Stud Book. However, the registry does not stipulate the percentages of these strains, and consequently there is no standard of type.

The best Anglo-Arabs, combining the speed, substance, and conformation of the Thoroughbred with the intelligence, soundness, stamina, and equability of the Arab, make excellent show jumpers, eventers, dressage horses, show hacks, and hunters.

Anglo-Arab (French)

In the early nineteenth century, native mares of southwestern France, already improved in the past by infusions of oriental blood, were mated with Arab and English Thoroughbred stallions (and subsequently also with Anglo-Arabs) to produce the type formerly known as the *Demi-sang du Midi* or Southern Part-Bred. Until quite recently a distinction was made between this and the purebred Anglo-Arab (50 percent of each race), but both are now registered in the same stud book. The minimum accepted percentage of Arab blood is 25 percent.

Anglo-Arabs have consistently been bred on more systematic lines in France than in England, largely because of the influence of the national studs at Pompadour, Tarbes, and Pau. By alternately using Thoroughbred and Arab stallions in successive generations, the characteristics of neither breed become predominant.

Usually bay or chestnut, the Anglo-Arab stands 14.3 to 16.2 hands (sometimes more). It has a fine, straight-profiled head with large, wide-set eyes, a deep chest, oblique shoulders, a short, well-shaped back, and sound legs and feet.

▲ Anglo-Norman ▼ Appaloosa

Anglo-Norman

Because of its favorable climate and fertile soil, Normandy has always been one of France's important horse-breeding areas. During the seventeenth century imported stallions were used to improve the native breed; in the 1830s this was systematically crossed with English half-breds, and later with Thoroughbreds and trotters, to produce the Anglo-Norman. At first these half-breds were used as coach horses and trotters, but with increasing motorization they provided army remounts and, eventually, saddlehorses. In the nineteenth century the Anglo-Norman had already been used in western and central France to produce the Vendéen-Charentais and the Charollais saddlehorses. All three types, now grouped under the general name *Selle français* (French Saddlehorse), are excellent riding horses, the Anglo-Norman being particularly successful as a show jumper.

Standing about 16 hands, the Anglo-Norman is normally bay or chestnut. It has a medium-sized head with rather long ears, a long, muscular neck, compact body with powerful shoulders and quarters, and hard limbs.

Appaloosa

The early development of this American breed of spotted horse is attributed to the Nez Percé Indians, who inhabited the region bordering the Palouse River (hence, Appaloosa) in the northwest. The foundation stock, mainly of Spanish origin, is believed to have come from Mexico and South America. By careful selective breeding the type was later stabilized into a breed, which was accorded official recognition in 1938, with the formation of the Appaloosa Horse Club.

The normal height of the Appaloosa is 14 to 15.3 hands, although there is no maximum limit. The forehand may be of any color, while the hindquarters must be white with round or oval spots of the same color as the forehand. In the white Appaloosa, the whole coat is white and spots of any other color are distributed over the entire body. The six basic patterns are known as frost, leopard, marble, snowflake, spotted blanket, and white blanket. Other distinctive characteristics of the breed are a wispy mane and tail, mottled pinkish-gray skin, prominent whites around the eyes, and vertically striped hoofs. **57**

Arab

A breed of great antiquity and outstanding beauty, the Arab, originally fostered by the Bedouins of Arabia, is now established in 40 different countries. Most, if not all, warm-blood breeds were either originally based on the Arab or have at some time been improved by the introduction, direct or indirect, of Arab blood.

Normally standing 14 to 15 hands (although there are no height restrictions for the breed), the Arab is gray, chestnut, or bay and has a long, fine mane and tail. The wedge-shaped head, carried high on an arched neck, is concave in profile, with small ears, large, prominent eyes, large nostrils, and a small, soft muzzle. The body is well ribbed-up, with long, sloping shoulders, a broad, deep chest, short back, broad, level quarters, and a high-set tail. The hard limbs have well-defined tendons, large hocks, flat knees, and hard, round hoofs. At all paces the Arab has a free, fast action, and this, combined with its hardy constitution, courage, ability to carry weight, and lively yet tractable nature, make it a riding horse of quality and distinction.

Akhal-Teke

A direct descendant of the extinct Turkmene horse, the elegant Akhal-Teke is found principally in the Soviet Republic of Turkmenistan but is also bred in Kazakhstan, Kirghizia, and Uzbekistan. It is an extremely hardy animal, capable of existing under conditions of great heat and privation, and today is used mainly for racing, jumping, and dressage.

Standing about 15 hands, the Akhal-Teke is a light but strong-boned horse. It has a long, fine head with wide-set eyes, carried on a long, thin, high-set neck. Sloping shoulders, high withers, a narrow, rather shallow chest, and a long, strong back and loins are also characteristic. The limbs are long and, like the feet, very hard. Bay and chestnut are the predominant colors, but grays and duns also occur. The coat is very fine and sometimes bears a pronounced golden or silvery metallic sheen. The mane and tail are short, sparse, and silky.

Barb

Formerly known as the Barbary Horse, the Barb originated in North Africa—in Morocco, Algeria, Tunis, and Tripoli. Since the eighth century it has been crossed with Arabs (especially from Syria) and other eastern breeds to such an extent that purebred Barbs are now restricted almost exclusively to Morocco. During the seventeenth century the Barb was imported into Britain and Europe, where it was used in the foundation of a number of breeds, including the Thoroughbred.

The purebred Barb stands 14 to 15 hands and is bay, brown, chestnut, black, or gray, with a profuse mane and flowing, low-set tail. It is characterized by a relatively long head, flat shoulders, rounded chest, sloping croup, and well-made legs and feet. Like all desert-bred horses, the Barb has a very hardy constitution and is able to thrive on poor keep. It is particularly noted for its great speed over short distances.

Opposite, Royal Guard, Morocco; this page, Sahara Barbs in the Cameroons

Budeonny

Bred in the Ukraine and Rostov regions of the Soviet Union, the Budeonny was developed principally from Don and Thoroughbred stock and became an officially recognized breed in 1948.

Standing about 16 hands, it has a medium-sized head with a straight or slightly concave profile. A long, often arched neck and high withers are combined with a rounded body, long, sloping shoulders, a broad, relatively short back, and muscular quarters to produce a powerful, well-made horse. The limbs are strong, with clearly defined tendons and about 8 inches of bone below the knee. Chestnut is the predominant color, although bay, brown, and black are also common.

Budeonnys have a lively but equable temperament and are noted for their speed, stamina, and natural jumping ability. Originally bred mainly as cavalry horses, they are now used for sport, mostly steeple-chasing, show jumping, and dressage.

Cob

The term cob usually denotes a type (as opposed to a breed) of horse that is found throughout the British Isles but is most closely associated with Ireland and the west of England.

Not exceeding 15.3 hands (or 15.1 hands for showing purposes), the cob is a short-legged, stocky, rounded animal with the bone, substance, and weight-carrying capacity of a heavyweight hunter. It has a small, quality head, powerful, shapely neck (in the show ring set off by a hogged mane), deep girth, short, strong back, massive quarters, and hard, powerful legs.

In spite of its rather heavy appearance, the cob is not sluggish; it has a good, low, comfortable action at all paces and often shows exceptional balance, agility, and jumping ability. With its calm, sensible nature, it has proved a steady, reliable mount, ideal for inexperienced, heavy, or elderly riders.

Compare **Welsh Cob** (p. 106).

Criollo

The development of this South American breed is said to date back to 1536, when the Spanish explorer Pedro de Mendoza brought about 100 Spanish Andalusians into Argentina. With the sacking by the Indians of the newly founded Buenos Aires, many of these horses escaped into the Pampas. The extreme climatic conditions caused the survivors to evolve into very hardy animals later tamed by settlers for use as cattle- and pack-horses.

About a hundred years ago the breed was almost destroyed by constant crossing with imported stallions from Europe and the United States, which undermined its hardiness and natural resistance to disease. Fortunately it was gradually reestablished by a program of strict selective breeding, using only the best remaining stock.

Now bred in Argentina, Brazil, and Peru, the Criollo stands about 14 hands and is normally dun. A tough, agile, long-lived animal with great powers of endurance, it has a short head, muscular shoulders, a short, straight back, strong, rounded quarters, and hard legs.

Furioso

The Hungarian Furioso takes its name from the founder stallion, an English Thoroughbred by Privateer, foaled in 1836 and imported into Hungary about 1840. From 1841 to 1851 he sired 95 colt foals, which were sent to studs throughout Austro-Hungary. British stock was later imported to strengthen the breed, and a second line was founded by the stallion North Star (foaled in 1844). These two half-bred families have since become so closely intermingled that they are now frequently regarded as one breed, the Furioso-North Star.

Standing about 16 hands, the Furioso is usually black or dark brown. An elegant, robust, well-made saddlehorse, it has a breedy head carried on a shapely neck, high withers, sloping shoulders, well-muscled quarters, and strong legs. It is used in many equestrian sports, including racing, steeplechasing, dressage, show jumping, and eventing. The breed is also found in Czechoslovakia, Poland, and Rumania.

▲ Criollo; below and left, Furioso

Hack

A type, as opposed to a breed, of high-class riding horse, the hack is associated almost exclusively with the show ring. The qualities prized in the modern show hack are refinement, elegance, and grace combined with perfect manners, true, low movements, and extremely good conformation.

At most sizable shows in Britain hacks are divided into two classes: large hacks (over 15 hands but not exceeding 15.3 hands); and small hacks (up to 15 hands). Small hack classes in general show less uniformity of type and are usually of a lower standard. In theory, hacks may be of any breed or mixture of breeds. In practice, however, most successful large hacks are Thoroughbreds, or have a very high percentage of Thoroughbred blood in their breeding, while small hacks are often bred up from pony mares crossed with Thoroughbred, Arab, or Anglo-Arab stallions.

Hanoverian

The development of the modern Hanoverian dates from the early eighteenth century, when George, Elector of Hanover, became king of England. Close contact became established between British and Hanoverian breeders, and the Hanoverian horse, used at that time in agriculture and as a carriage horse, was improved by the regular use of imported Thoroughbred stallions. Toward the end of the nineteenth century, crossing with blood horses was reduced to a minimum as the offspring were said to be too light for agricultural use. After World War II there was an increasing demand for riding as opposed to harness horses, and the breed was modified by the further use of Thoroughbreds and also by infusions of Trakehner blood.

Today the Hanoverian, a strong, elegant, well-made animal standing 16 to 17 hands, has a worldwide reputation as a show jumper. It is also used for hunting, combined training, dressage, and other equestrian sports.

Holstein

With a history said to trace back to the fourteenth century, the Holstein was originally developed as a warhorse in the marshlands bordering the Elbe River. The foundation stock is believed to have consisted of indigenous horses, which were crossed with oriental, Spanish, and Neapolitan stallions.

During the nineteenth century imported Yorkshire Coach and Thoroughbred stallions were introduced, and the Holstein evolved into a dual-purpose coach/artillery and riding horse. More recently, extensive use was made of Thoroughbred blood to produce a strong, quality saddlehorse, which has proved particularly suitable for jumping and combined training.

Standing up to 16.2 hands and usually bay, bay-brown, or black, the Holstein has a long, straight head set on a strong, well-shaped neck. The body is muscular and compact with a deep chest, short back, and powerful loins and quarters; the legs are shortish, with muscular forearms and about 9½ inches of bone below the knee.

Hunter

A distinction is made between the field hunter, a horse that is regularly hunted and is judged in show classes purely for performance and soundness, and the conformation hunter, which is judged both for conformation and performance but is seldom actually hunted.

The field hunter may be of any breed or mixture of breeds; it is selected primarily for its working qualities and suitability for the country in which it is to be ridden. The conformation hunter, however, is much more uniform in type. Usually Thoroughbred or near-Thoroughbred, it stands 15 to 17 hands and may be of any color. Prized qualities are a well-proportioned head and neck, a deep, powerful body with sloping shoulders, short back, strong loins, a short croup, and well-developed quarters. The legs must be strong, with good joints, short cannons, and at least 8 inches of dense bone (10 inches for heavyweight hunters); the feet should be hard and open.

All hunters must have a free, true action at the walk and trot, but above all they must be able to sustain a long, low, effortless gallop. **69**

Anglo-Kabardin

Considered the best of all mountain riding horses, the Anglo-Kabardin is the product of crossing Kabardin mares with English Thoroughbred stallions. It was bred and developed in the Stavropol region and the Kabardin Republic of the U.S.S.R.

Standing about 15 hands, the Anglo-Kabardin is strongly built, with good conformation. It has an excellent reputation and shows extreme endurance and very good action. It is now used to improve other breeds in the Caucasus.

Kabardin

A mountain breed from the northern Caucasus, the Kabardin is believed
to have resulted from the crossing of eastern steppe horses with Persians,
Turkmenes, Karabakhs, and Arabs from the south.

It is a strong, well-built animal, normally bay but sometimes dark
brown, black, or gray. The head is convex in profile with long ears
pointing inward at the tip; the neck is strong and muscular; the back is
rather long. The stout, relatively short legs have hard tendons and tough,
regularly formed hoofs, although there is a tendency toward sickle
hocks. The average height of stallions is 15.0½ hands and of mares,
14.2½ hands.

Long-lived and extremely fertile, the Kabardin is noted for its calm,
sensible nature, great agility, sure-footedness, and stamina. It provides a
reliable means of mountain transport and is also used locally for racing
and various sports.

71

Karabakh

A mountain breed of ancient origin, the Karabakh is native to the Karabakh mountains in the Soviet republic of Azerbaijan. It has been identified by some authorities with the Karadagh from the neighboring province of Azerbaidzhan, in northwestern Iran.

Standing 14.1 to 14.3 hands, the Karabakh has a fine-textured coat, which is chestnut, bay, dun, or gray, often with the golden metallic sheen characteristic of several Russian breeds. It has a small, fine head with a prominent forehead, large eyes, and a small muzzle; a compact, powerful body with flat shoulders and strong, clean legs with hard, blue hoofs.

This elegant, even-tempered, energetic riding horse has a good action at all paces; it has had a considerable influence on a number of southern breeds, notably the Don.

Knabstrup

The history of this Danish breed of spotted horse is reputed to date back to the Napoleonic wars. Spanish soldiers stationed in Denmark are said to have left behind a chestnut mare with "blanket" markings and a white mane and tail. This mare was put to a Fredericksborg stallion and produced a spotted foal, "Flaebehingsten," which became the founder sire of the breed.

The average height of the Knabstrup was about 15.3 hands and in conformation it was very similar to, though somewhat lighter than, the Fredericksborg. Like the Appaloosa and other spotted horses, it has always been very popular as a circus and parade horse. Today the breed in its pure form is said to be virtually extinct, and many so-called Knabstrup horses are of very mixed descent.

Lipizzaner

Famed for its association with the Spanish Riding School in Vienna, this breed takes its name from Lipizza, near Trieste. Here, in 1580, a stud was founded by Archduke Karl, using largely Spanish stock, to provide horses for the imperial court. After the dissolution of the Austro-Hungarian empire, the Austrian share of the stud was moved to its present home, Piber, in Styria. All the stallions used in the Vienna school are bred there, returning later for stud duties if they have proved themselves in the school.

Standing 14.2 to 15 hands, Lipizzaners are usually gray, with a sleek coat and a silky mane and tail. They have a fine head with large eyes, small ears, and wide nostrils; a strong neck, heavy shoulders, and a well-muscled body with a longish back. The legs are strong and slender, with small, hard feet.

Because of their quick intelligence and gentle, willing disposition, Lipizzaners are particularly suitable for any kind of work involving a high degree of training. Added to this they have a proud bearing and a naturally high, spectacular action.

▲ "Capriole at the Hand" ▼ "Levade under the rider"

Lusitano

The Lusitano, which resembles the Spanish Andalusian and is believed to be related to it, is an ancient breed of Portugal. It was formerly favored by the army as a remount and was also used for light agricultural work. Today, although the number of purebred animals is declining, Lusitanos are still used in mounted bullfighting—a sport requiring intelligent, highly trained horses with exceptional agility and speed.

Standing 14.3 to 15.3 hands, the Lusitano may be of any solid color, although gray is most common. It has a fairly short, thick neck with a full mane, a compact body with strong shoulders, sloping croup with a profuse, slightly low-set tail, and long legs with small hoofs. There is an occasional tendency for horses of this breed to have a heavy, rather unattractive head, with long ears and a Roman nose.

Shagya Arab

This famous Arab half-bred strain, now found in the United States as well as throughout Europe, was originally developed at the Babolna stud in Hungary. The founder sire, from which it takes its name, was an Arab of the Saglawi strain, foaled in about 1830 and imported from Syria in 1836.

Standing about 15 hands, the Shagya is usually gray with a silky mane and tail, and a fine coat. Its small, fine head, which has a straight or slightly concave profile, is carried on a graceful, arched neck. The body is deep and well rounded, with strong loins and quarters, a flat croup, and a high-set tail. The limbs are slender and strong, with about 7¼ inches of bone below the knee and small, hard feet.

Like the Arab itself, the Shagya is an extremely beautiful, but also very hardy, animal of great stamina. Although primarily a saddlehorse, it is sometimes used in eastern Europe for light draft purposes. **77**

Mustang

When the Spanish first landed in America, there were no native horses. The early equine population consisted entirely of Spanish stock, introduced first by Cortés into Mexico and later by Coronado and others into the southwestern states. Some of these horses strayed, or were taken by the Indians and subsequently escaped, to form the nucleus of vast feral herds that rapidly spread all over the plains of North America.

Large numbers were caught both by Indians and white settlers, and toward the end of the nineteenth century mustangs were being rounded up in their hundreds for breaking to saddle or harness. In most states there was no law to protect the breed, and until the 1950s whole herds were being slaughtered for dog food. As a result, the mustang population, which numbered over 2 million in 1900, now stands at less than 7,000. Fortunately, in 1971, a law was passed giving nationwide protection to this small, tough, wiry horse.

Palomino

Recognized as a color breed in the United States, and a color type elsewhere, the Palomino is characterized by a golden coat (described as the color of a newly minted gold coin) and a silvery-white mane and tail. Under the registration requirements of both the Palomino Horse Association and the Palomino Horse Breeders of America, the coat must be of a uniform color with no light or dark patches of hair on the body, no zebra stripes, and no white markings except on the face and lower leg. The eyes must be dark (wall or blue eyes are unacceptable), and no more than 15 percent of the hairs in the mane and tail may be of a darker tone. The majority of registered Palominos in the United States are either Quarter Horses or Saddlebreds.

The crossings most likely to produce this coloration are between Palomino and Palomino, Palomino and chestnut, Palomino and Albino, or chestnut and Albino.

Persian Arab

It has long been claimed by the Iranians—and some notable authorities subscribe to this theory—that the Persian Arab is a direct descendant of the forebears of the Arab horse and is, therefore, the older breed. The two breeds share many common characteristics, but the Persian Arab is usually taller, and its fine head, although having the same large eyes, neat prick ears, and small muzzle as the Arab, is not dished in profile.

Like the Arab, it is an arrestingly beautiful animal. Normally gray, bay, chestnut, more rarely black, it has an arched neck, a light, well-muscled body with a short back and high-set tail, and fine, strong limbs with small, hard hoofs. The breed is noted for its speed, agility, and great stamina.

Pinto

The Pinto, or Paint Horse, is characterized by a two-colored coat consisting of clearly defined areas of white and either black, bay, brown, or (more rarely) dun or roan. There are two basic coat patterns. The tobiano has a predominantly white coat with large patches of the darker color distributed mainly on the head, neck, flanks, and chest. The overo shows splashes of white (particularly on the midsection of the body but also on the face) on a basically dark coat. In the overo the legs are frequently dark and the white rarely extends across the back; the reverse is true of the tobiano.

Since the formation in 1962 of the American Paint Horse Association (APHA), great progress has been made toward establishing a fixed type modeled along stockhorse lines. To qualify for entry to the Association's registry, all horses foaled since 1969 must have one parent registered in the regular or breeding-stock registry, while the other, if not in the APHA listings, must be a registered Quarter Horse or Thoroughbred. The minimum height requirement is 14 hands and gaited horses are not accepted.

Tersk

One of the most recent Russian breeds, granted official recognition in 1948, the Tersk was developed during the 1920s. It was bred at the Stavropol and Tersk studs in the northern Caucasus from a foundation stock of Strelets horses, Arabs, Kabardins, and Dons. A hardy, good-natured animal with a free, graceful action at all paces, the Tersk is particularly suitable for sport, especially steeplechasing, cross-country, and dressage. It is also used for a variety of other purposes, both under saddle and in harness.

Standing about 15 hands, the Tersk is commonly gray, with a fine coat and a silky mane and tail. It has a medium-sized head, usually straight but sometimes slightly dished in profile, with large eyes and long, erect ears. The neck is fairly long and well shaped, and the body is compact and round-ribbed, with sloping shoulders, wide loins, and a flat croup. The legs are fine with 7¼ to 7¾ inches of flat bone below the knee.

Polo Pony

Polo was introduced to the west from India. The game was taken up in the 1850s by British planters in Assam and later by the army. From England it rapidly spread to other parts of the former British Empire, to the United States, and to Argentina. In 1886 international polo started with the first of the Anglo-American Westchester Cup matches.

Native or local ponies were originally used for the game. Later, as the height limit (originally set at 13.2 hands in India) was steadily raised and finally abolished, breeders aimed at producing a specialized

Thoroughbred type. In Argentina imported Thoroughbred stallions were used very successfully from about 1900 to upgrade local stock, and since World War II Argentinian ponies and players have remained supreme.

Normally 14.2 to 16 hands (15.1 hands is regarded as the optimum height), polo ponies should have a long, flexible neck, deep, broad chest, good shoulders, a strong back with well-sprung ribs, powerful quarters, and hard legs and feet. They must also possess speed, agility, stamina, courage, balance, and an eager but not overexcitable temperament.

▲ Quarter Horse ▼ Oldenburg

Quarter Horse

The history of the Quarter Horse dates back to colonial days in the Carolinas and Virginia, where match racing, usually over distances of about 440 yards, was a popular sport. The competing horses (quarter-milers) were developed from local ponies—descendants of animals introduced by Spanish settlers—crossed with imported English stock. Quarter Horses were also used for all kinds of work, both under saddle and in harness. With the opening up of the West, they proved invaluable as cow-ponies, combining speed and agility with weight, strength, inherent "cow-sense," and an excellent temperament. Today, the uses of this versatile breed include ranching, racing, hunting, trail-riding, polo, and jumping.

Quarter Horses may be of any solid color. They have a short, broad head carried low on a slightly arched neck, which blends into strong, deep-sloping shoulders. The body is close-coupled and muscular, with a deep, broad chest, short back, and massive quarters. The legs are short with muscular forearms, short cannons, and strong, open, rounded hoofs.

Oldenburg

Originally based on the Friesian, the Oldenburg was improved in the latter part of the eighteenth century by the use of imported Barb, English half-bred, Neapolitan, and Spanish stallions. About a hundred years later, the breed was further modified by the introduction of Cleveland Bay, Norman, Hanoverian, and Thoroughbred blood. The resultant strong, utility-type horse remained unchanged until after World War II. Breeders then began to develop it for riding purposes, importing the Norman stallion Condor in 1950, and since then, Hanoverians, Thoroughbreds, and Trakehners.

The largest of the German warm-blood breeds, the Oldenburg stands 16.2 to 17.2 hands and is normally brown, bay, or black. It has a large, plain head, short, thick neck, and a strong, deep body with pronounced muscular shoulders and powerful quarters. The legs are short and sturdy with strong joints and plenty of bone. The hocks are well let-down, and the hoofs are hard, if sometimes rather flat. Oldenburgs mature early, have a good action, and are said to be fertile and long-lived.

Swedish Warm-Blood

This horse was originally bred to provide remounts for the army. Imported stallions of various warm-blood breeds, notably Hanoverians, Trakehners, and Thoroughbreds, were crossed with local horses, which had already been improved by the introduction in the seventeenth century of oriental, Spanish, and Friesian blood.

Strong, compact, good-looking animals with excellent conformation, Swedish Warm-Blood horses stand about 16.2 hands and are normally bay, brown, chestnut, or gray. Because of their placid, sensible nature and outstanding action, they have proved particularly suitable for dressage. They hold an impressive record of international and Olympic successes not only in this discipline, but also in show jumping and eventing.

The breed has been exported in considerable numbers to the United States, as well as to Britain, West Germany, and Switzerland.

Tennessee Walking Horse

This breed, also known as the Plantation Walking Horse or Turn-Row, was developed in Tennessee in the 1850s as a comfortable means of transport for plantation owners, who had to spend many hours in the saddle. Its mixed parentage includes Canadian and Narragansett Pacers, Morgan, Saddlebred, Standardbred, and Thoroughbred blood.

The most distinctive feature of this horse is its unique *running walk,* a very smooth and comfortable gliding, four-beat gait said never to have been taught successfully to any other breed.

Walkers are now bred mainly as show and pleasure horses. They stand 15.2 to 16 hands and occur in a variety of colors, including sorrel, bay-brown, chestnut, black, and roan, often with white markings. They have a long, straight-profiled head, carried high on a powerful neck that blends into deep-sloping shoulders. The body is solid and muscular, with a deep chest, short back, and slightly sloping quarters; the legs are clean and hard. Both the mane and tail (which for showing purposes is usually artificially set) are very full.

Thoroughbred

The development of this breed dates from the post-Restoration period in England, when racing became a popular sport. The official founder sires, to which all Thoroughbreds trace in the male line, were the Byerley Turk (imported 1689), the Darley Arabian (1704), and the Godolphin Arabian (1728). Some of the foundation mares, too, were imported Arabs, but it is believed that many were drawn from native racing stock.

The normal height range for Thoroughbreds is 15 to 17 hands; the coat is fine and may be of any solid color. Thoroughbreds have a refined head, long, arched neck, pronounced withers, and sloping shoulders. The body is deep, with well-sprung ribs, a short back, and sloping croup; the legs are clean, with long forearms, short cannons, and pronounced tendons.

Thoroughbreds are now raced in over 50 countries, including the United States, which was the first country outside Britain and Ireland to breed them and now has the largest racing and bloodstock industry in the world. Elsewhere Thoroughbreds have been widely used as foundation stock and to improve native breeds.

Trakehner

Now bred principally in West Germany and Poland, the Trakehner originated in East Prussia. Its development was closely associated with the Trakehnen Stud in the northwestern part of the province, founded by Friedrich Wilhelm I in 1732. The breed was based on the native Schweiken, a small active horse of ancient origin, which from the beginning of the nineteenth century was crossed with imported Arabs and English Thoroughbred stallions.

Elegant, good-natured animals, noted for their sound constitution and stamina, Trakehners stand between 16 and 16.2 hands and may be of any solid color. They have a breedy head, well ribbed-up body with a deep chest, sloping shoulders, a short, strong back, sloping croup and powerful quarters, and hard legs and feet. They have proved particularly suitable for dressage and show jumping and have been used both in Europe and America for improving native stock.

Turkoman

Found in northern Iran, this breed of hardy desert horse is closely related to the Akhal-Teke and Jomud of the Soviet Union; all three breeds are descended from the extinct Turkmene horse.

Standing 15 to 15.2 hands, it is normally gray, bay, chestnut, or dun and has a fine-textured coat and a silky, rather sparse mane and tail. It has a medium-sized head, broad between the eyes and tapering to a small, narrow muzzle; a long, thin neck (horses of this breed tend to be ewe-necked), high, prominent withers, a narrow chest, a fairly short back, and a sloping croup. The legs are long and fine with well-defined tendons and small, hard, rounded hoofs. The Turkoman is noted for its speed, strength, and stamina—qualities that have made it particularly successful in long-distance races and endurance tests—and also for its unique ''floating'' action.

Waler

To produce stockhorses that could also serve for general saddle and light harness purposes, early Australian settlers crossed imported stallions (mainly Thoroughbreds, but Arabs and Anglo-Arabs were also used) with the best available mares. The mares, too, were imported or derived from imported stock and are thought to have included Cape horses from South Africa and cob, pony, and draft types of European origin. This resulted in the emergence of a distinct type, the Waler, which rapidly gained a reputation for toughness and endurance. From 1850 to 1930 regular shipments of Walers were sent to the Indian Army, and during World War I they were in great demand as remounts and artillery horses. The demand subsequently declined, although Waler-type horses continued to be bred at many sheep and cattle stations. An official register has now been opened with the object of transforming the type into a fixed breed—the Australian Stockhorse.

Horses of the Waler type usually stand 14.2 to 16 hands. They have a deep, well ribbed-up body with prominent withers, sloping shoulders, a strong back, muscular quarters, and good legs.

Cleveland Bay

This long-established British breed of obscure origin is native to the Cleveland district of North Yorkshire. As the name suggests, it is invariably bay in color, with black points; the only acceptable white marking is a small star. It has a large head with a slightly convex profile, a long neck, and a deep, wide muscular body with low withers, strong loins, and long, powerful quarters. The legs are relatively short, hard, and clean, with 8½ to 9½ inches of hard, flat bone below the knee. Clevelands tend to mature late, usually reaching their full height (15.2 to 16.2 hands) at about five or six years of age. They are, however, correspondingly long-lived and are notably fertile and prepotent.

Formerly used in agriculture, for pack and haulage work, and as coach horses and hunters, Clevelands are now bred mainly for crossing with Thoroughbreds to produce show jumpers, hunters, and event horses. The breed has also been exported as an improver.

Don

The Old Don was a small, tough, very active horse that inhabited the steppes and plains bordering the Don River. It had at various times been improved by infusions of Karabakh, Persian, Turkmene, and other blood. During the nineteenth century these horses were crossed with Orlovs and Thoroughbreds to produce the Don horse known today.

A good-natured, well-made, exceptionally hardy animal, it stands 15.1 to 15.3 hands and may be of any solid color, although at one time golden chestnuts predominated. It has a medium-sized head, straight in profile; a well-developed chest, straight, broad back, solid loins, and a long, broad croup. The legs are long, with 7½ to 8 inches of bone below the knee, and the hoofs are large and very hard. The breed is used both under saddle and in harness. It provided the foundation for the Budeonny and has been widely used as an improver in the Soviet Union.

Carthusian

The Andalusian Carthusian horse of today owes its purity of strain to its developers, the Carthusian monks. These clerics began and maintained excellent herds of Oriental origin, which were not crossed with foreign blood. In the seventeenth and eighteenth centuries, in an effort to breed larger animals, royal edict introduced new blood in the form of heavy stallions from Denmark, Holland, and Naples. The monks of Jerez, however, disregarded this and continued to use only African or Asiatic stallions. The modern studs of Terry and Salvatierra have lines to the original Carthusian horses.

Originally the color was chestnut or black, but about 50 years ago two gray stallions were bred into the line and the breed is now predominantly gray.

East Friesian

A German breed, originally small, sturdy, and rather heavy, the East Friesian was developed along the same lines as the neighboring Oldenburg (see p. 77). Over the years it was similarly modified to conform to the breeding standards and requirements of the day by the use of outside blood of various kinds. After World War II Arab stallions from the Marbach stud were used, bringing about a further change in type; more recently considerable amounts of Hanoverian blood have been introduced with a view to producing a quality multi-purpose horse of the kind now required.

Of any solid color, the East Friesian is a strong, well-muscled, deep-bodied animal with a fine head, fairly long, arched neck, and shortish, sturdy limbs.

Gelderland

Associated chiefly with the Dutch provinces of Gelderland, Utrecht, and North and South Holland, the Gelderland was developed from native mares crossed with stallions of widely differing origin. In the early 1800s these included horses from Britain, Egypt, Germany, Hungary, Poland, and Russia; later East Friesians and Oldenburgs were used. At the beginning of the twentieth century Hackneys and Anglo-Normans were introduced and the latter continue to be used today.

The Gelderland stands about 16 hands and is commonly chestnut with white markings. It has a clean-cut head and strong, shapely neck, and its deep, muscular body has long, sloping shoulders, a long, sometimes slightly drooping croup, and a high-set tail. The legs are strong and well muscled.

Although the breed is still worked on farms, Gelderlands are being used increasingly for pleasure, especially driving, for which their stylish action and proud carriage make them particularly suited. Breeders are now crossing Gelderlands with Holstein, Trakehner, and English Thoroughbred and half-bred stallions to obtain a type more suitable for riding.

Karabair

A breed of ancient and uncertain origin, the Karabair is found principally in Uzbekistan, in the Soviet Union, where it is used both under saddle and in harness. It is a hardy animal, noted for its great strength, agility, speed, and endurance, and is well adapted for work in a hot, dry climate.

Although less fine than the Arab, the Karabair resembles this breed in size and conformation. It stands 14.2 to 15.1 hands and is commonly gray, bay, or chestnut, with a fine coat and sparse mane and tail. The head is medium sized, with a straight profile and large, prominent eyes. Karabairs have a short, thick neck, high withers, wide chest, a straight and usually fairly short back, and a broad, powerful croup. The legs are hard, with strong tendons and 7 to 7¾ inches of bone below the knee, and the hoofs are small, strong, and upright.

East Bulgarian

Development of the East Bulgarian breed began at the end of the nineteenth century at the former Kabijuk Stud (now part of the Vassil Kolarov State Agricultural Farm), near Shumen. The foundation stock consisted of local Arab, Anglo-Arab, and half-bred English mares, which were crossed with imported Thoroughbred or half-bred stallions and, to a lesser extent, with Arabs.

A strong, hardy, active horse with good conformation, the East Bulgarian stands about 15.3 hands and is usually chestnut or black. It is used in harness for farm work and also for general riding and competitive sports. Horses of this breed have competed at international level in show jumping and dressage and have an outstanding record as steeplechasers.

Morgan

It is claimed that the ancestry of this breed can be traced directly to a compact bay stallion of 14.2 hands, believed to have been sired by True Briton, a Thoroughbred racehorse. Foaled in about 1790, he was originally called Figure but became better known as Justin Morgan, after his second owner, an innkeeper of Vermont. As well as being worked on the land, he was raced and offered at stud. As a sire he proved extremely prepotent, passing on to his offspring not only his conformation but also his exceptional stamina and speed. By the time he died in 1821 he had established one of the most popular and versatile breeds in the United States.

Standing 14 to 15 hands, the Morgan is usually bay and has a profuse mane and tail. The head, carried high on a thick, crested neck, is straight in profile, with small ears and wide-set eyes. The body is compact and well rounded, with a deep, broad chest, muscular, sloping shoulders, a short back, and powerful quarters. The tail is set low but carried well, and the legs are fine and strong with plenty of bone.

Novokirghiz

This hardy mountain breed, officially recognized in 1954, was developed in the Soviet Union from the native Kirghiz—a small, hardy breed of ancient origin, improved by earlier random crossings. In an intensive program started in about 1930, Kirghiz mares were crossed with Thoroughbred and other stallions. The resultant Anglo-Kirghiz mares were crossed with Dons, Anglo-Dons, and Kirghiz-Dons. The best of the progeny were then interbred, and the most suitable stallions were crossed with Don-Kirghiz and Anglo-Kirghiz mares, thus finally establishing the Novokirghiz.

Usually standing 14.2 to 15 hands, the Novokirghiz is bay, chestnut, or gray. It has a broad, muscular body and powerful, relatively short legs with well-developed joints and hard hoofs. This good-looking, sure-footed, normally docile animal shows a good, lively action at all paces. The breed is suitable both for work under saddle and in harness and is also used for sport and transport.

Standardbred

The name Standardbred dates back to 1879, when, in order to be entered in the American Trotting Registry, trotters and pacers had to comply with a one-mile speed standard.

The official founder sire was Messenger, a gray Thoroughbred imported into Philadelphia in about 1788. The strongest influence on the breed, however, came from one of his great-grandsons, Hambletonian 10, or Rysdyk's Hambletonian, foaled in 1849. Between 1851 and 1875 he sired 1,331 foals, and the majority of present-day Standardbreds can be traced back to him.

Although a number of breeds, including the Arab, Barb, Cleveland Bay, Hackney, and Morgan, are said to have contributed to its make-up, the Standardbred is richest in Thoroughbred blood. In conformation, the two breeds are basically very similar but the Standardbred tends to be smaller and is more robust in appearance, with a longer body and shorter legs.

Lokai

A small but very strong, hardy, and agile mountain breed, the Lokai is found in Tadzhikistan in the Soviet Union. Here it is used primarily for pack and saddle work but also for racing and various other equestrian sports. The breed is reputed to have been developed during the sixteenth century from native Mongol stock, with later infusions of Jomud, Karabair, and Arab blood.

Normally reaching a height of about 14.2 hands, the Lokai has a short head with a broad forehead and a straight or slightly convex profile, carried on a straight neck of medium length. The body is compact and close-coupled, with a well-developed chest, short, straight back, short, muscular loins, and a drooping croup. The legs are strong and have good bone and joints, although there is a tendency toward sickle hocks. The coat, which may be bay, gray, chestnut, or (more rarely) black or dun, sometimes has a tight, curly texture. The mane and tail are usually rather sparse.

Welsh Cob

This horse is virtually a larger version of the Welsh pony of cob type (see p. 44). Although the precise origins of the breed are unknown, some authorities believe that it descended from native stock crossed in the twelfth century with imported Spanish warhorses.

Normally between 14 and 15.1 hands, the Welsh Cob may be any color except piebald or skewbald; the predominant colors are bay, brown, black, chestnut, and roan. It has a small, quality head, a shapely neck, and a strong, deep body with a broad chest and long, massive quarters. The legs are sturdy and relatively short, sometimes with a little silky feather on the heels, and the hoofs are hard and well shaped.

Welsh Cobs are exceptionally strong, nimble animals with a bold, free action and considerable jumping ability. These qualities, combined with their gentle disposition, make them ideal as family mounts and hunters. They also take readily to harness and are invaluable for general ride-and-drive purposes.

Wielkopolski

The Wielkopolski was created by crossing local mares with eastern and Trakehner stallions. Until the development of the modern breed, there existed throughout central and western Poland a number of dual-purpose horses, which were officially recognized as separate breeds. These included the Poznan, which was based on Arab, Hanoverian, Thoroughbred, and Trakehner blood, and the Masuren, which was developed at the Liski stud after World War II. Although these older breeds no longer officially exist, distinct regional types are still evident within the Wielkopolski breed itself.

Wielkopolskis are generally large, handsome, well-made animals, equally suitable for use under saddle or in harness. They are said to mature early and are noted for their willing, amenable disposition and good action. **107**

Above and right, French Trotter ▼ Württemberg

French Trotter

The first trotting race in France was held in 1836, at Cherbourg, and the development of the French Trotter dates from the same period. Normandy breeders crossed mares of the native breed (which had already been improved in the seventeenth century by infusions of Arab, German, and other blood) with English half-bred hunters. Subsequently English Thoroughbreds and Norfolk Trotters were used, and at the end of the nineteenth century both racing trotters and coach horses were being bred from this stock. Other blood, including Orlov and American, was later introduced, but after 1941 the stud book excluded all but the offspring of previously registered sires and dams. Today trotting in France is unique in that there are still a number of races under saddle.

The French Trotter may be of any solid color, often with white markings. It stands about 16 hands and has high withers, fairly straight shoulders, a strong, short back, and hard limbs.

Württemberg

Bred principally at the Marbach stud in West Germany, founded in the late sixteenth century, the Württemberg was developed specifically as a working horse for use on farms in the area. It was based on local warm-blood mares, which were crossed initially with Arabs and later with various other stallions, including East Prussians, Normans, and Anglo-Normans.

The Württemberg is a hardy, tractable, well-built animal with a straight, squarish head set on a shapely neck of medium length. The body is deep and well ribbed-up, with powerful shoulders and loins, and the legs are strong, with plenty of bone below the knee and hard hoofs. The average height of the breed is about 16 hands, and the predominant colors are chestnut, brown, bay, and black, often with white markings on the face and limbs. **109**

▲ Nonius ▼ Kladruber

Nonius

The Nonius originated in Hungary and takes its name from the founder stallion, an Anglo-Norman taken during the Napoleonic Wars by Hungarian cavalrymen to the Mezohegyes stud in Hungary. There he was mated with Anglo-Norman and other stock, and sired 216 foals.

The Nonius tends to mature late (usually at about six years of age), but is correspondingly long-lived. It is normally black or brown and has a well-proportioned, breedy head, a long neck, high withers, strong shoulders and quarters, and hard limbs. There are two types, the smaller standing about 14.2 hands; the larger reaching 16 hands or so. They are both used in harness and also in agriculture.

Kladruber

The stud at Kladruby-on-Elbe, Czechoslovakia was founded in 1562 by Emperor Maximilian II. Starting from a foundation stock of Spanish origin, the breed was developed to provide coach and parade horses for the imperial court in Vienna. By the nineteenth century all colors other than black and white (gray) had been bred out.

The modern Kladruber stands 16.2 to 17.2 hands. This handsome, well-made animal is usually white and has a fine coat and a silky, flowing mane and tail. The head, which is convex in profile, is carried high on a strong, arched neck. The body is compact and rounded, with well-developed shoulders and quarters; the legs are strong and clean with good joints, well-defined tendons, and hard hoofs.

▲ German Trotter ▼ Hackney

German Trotter

Interest in harness racing developed in Germany toward the end of the nineteenth century. The first trotting club, the Altona of Hamburg, was formed in 1874, and in 1885 the first German trotter stud was founded, using Orlovs imported from Russia. These animals were greatly improved by crossing with American trotters; more recently, French blood has been introduced. Much of the breeding today is carried out at small farms with no more than one or two mares.

The German Trotter is a handsome, well-made animal and is noted for its even, tractable nature. It has a deep, broad chest, powerful, well-developed shoulders, a fairly long body with muscular loins and quarters, and strong, sturdy legs.

Hackney

The immediate ancestors of the Hackney, an English breed of high-stepping show horse, were the Norfolk Trotters, or Roadsters, of East Anglia. The best of these were descended from Shales, a half-bred son of Blaze, who in turn was by the famous racehorse Flying Childers, son of the Darley Arabian. Most modern Hackneys are descended from one of Shales' grandsons, Fireaway, foaled in about 1780.

Normally 14.3 to 15.3 hands, the Hackney is bay, brown, black, or chestnut, with a fine, silky coat and a full tail, which is set and carried high. It has a small head with a straight or convex profile, a muscular, crested neck, flat, powerful shoulders, and a compact body with well-sprung ribs. Its short legs are strong and clean, and the feet are round and fairly upright. At the trot the Hackney's action is extravagant and fluent, with the hind legs placed well under the body and the forelegs brought high at the knee and then thrown well forward.

Orlov

This Russian breed of trotter was developed by Count Alexei Orlov during the 1770s. He mated his Arab stallion Smetanka with a Danish mare, and their offspring, Polkan, was crossed with a Dutch mare to produce Bars I, the founder of the Orlov breed. Foaled in 1784, he was described as a tall, elegant animal with outstanding action, especially at the trot.

There are now said to be some 20 different bloodlines. Although these show considerable variation in conformation, the Orlov is basically a powerful, thickset animal with a strong constitution. Standing about 15.3 hands, it is gray, black, bay, or (more rarely) chestnut, with a profuse mane and tail. It normally has a fairly large, breedy head set on a long neck, a broad chest, long back, and strong legs with up to 8½ inches of bone below the knee and some feather on the fetlock.

Russian Trotter

During the nineteenth century it became apparent that the Orlov Trotter could not match the American trotter for speed. By the end of the century the breeding program that eventually produced the Russian Trotter was started. Standardbreds imported into the Soviet Union from the United States—totaling 156 stallions and 220 mares by the beginning of World War I—were crossed with Orlovs. The resultant crossbreds proved faster than the Orlov but were smaller and had poorer conformation. Subsequent efforts were concentrated chiefly on improving their size and conformation, and by the 1940s the program was completed. In 1949 the Russian Trotter, hitherto known as the Orlov-American crossbred, was officially established.

The Russian Trotter stands about 15.2 hands and is black, bay, brown, chestnut, or gray. It has a well-proportioned head with a straight or slightly convex profile, a long neck, powerful shoulders, deep broad chest, and sturdy legs with about 8 inches of bone below the knee.

Draft Horses

Comtois

An ancient breed, said to have descended from German horses imported by the Burgundians, the Comtois is found in eastern France in Franche-Comté—a rugged mountainous region comprising the departments of Doubs, Haute-Saône, and Jura.

Standing 14.3 to 15.3 hands and usually bay in color, the Comtois is a strong, hardy, very sure-footed animal, well adapted to work in the mountains. It has a square head, a straight neck, deep, compact body with good withers, and shortish, lightly feathered legs. It is inclined to be cow-hocked but has a good, lively action and great stamina.

Preceding pages: top left,
Percheron; bottom left, Suffolk
Punch; right, Shire.

Danubian

One of the three principal Bulgarian breeds, the Danubian was developed over a period of 40 to 50 years at the Georgi Dimitrov State Agricultural Farm, near Pleven. It was based on purebred Nonius stallions, which were crossed with mares of the Gidran strain to produce a strong, compact animal suitable for medium to heavy draft work.

Standing about 15.2 hands, the Danubian is black or dark chestnut, sometimes with white markings. Massive and solid, but not coarse, in its general appearance, it has a well-proportioned head set on a crested neck of medium length. The body is deep, broad, close-coupled, with strong quarters and a high-set tail; the legs are sturdy, with hard joints and hoofs. Although used primarily in harness, lighter specimens of the breed are sometimes ridden; Danubian mares crossed with Thoroughbred stallions often produce jumpers of quality.

Finnish

Developed from local native pony stock crossed with imported stallions of many breeds, both warm-blood and cold-blood, the Finnish horse has derived many useful qualities from its mixed parentage. It is a compact, long-lived animal, combining a quiet, willing temperament with surprising strength, speed, liveliness, and courage.

The breed is represented by two types. Both stand about 15.2 hands and are usually chestnut (although bays and blacks are occasionally seen), often with white markings. The lighter type, known as the Finnish Universal, weighs about 1,190 pounds and is used for riding, harness racing, and light transport, as well as for draft purposes. It is now far less common than the heavier draft type. Weighing about 1,270 pounds, this tough, resilient animal is used mainly in forestry and agriculture.

Fredericksborg

Developed at the Royal Fredericksborg Stud founded by Frederick II of Denmark in 1562, the Fredericksborg was bred principally from Spanish, Andalusian, and Neapolitan stock, with later infusions of Arab and Thoroughbred blood. It was soon regarded as one of the most elegant riding horses in Europe. The breed was in such great demand at all the courts that by 1839 the stud had to be disbanded because of the lack of suitable breeding stock. With the few remaining Fredericksborgs left in Denmark, a number of enthusiasts, notably in Seeland, continued the breed, but it is unlikely that the modern Fredericksborg much resembles the original.

The modern type is almost invariably chestnut. Standing about 15.3 hands, it is a strong, well-built animal with good conformation. Today the Fredericksborg is used mainly for light draft and harness work and for driving and riding.

Freiberger

Known also as the Franches Montagnes, this breed was developed in Switzerland toward the end of the nineteenth century. Local Jura mares were crossed with stallions of various breeds (notably Anglo-Normans), which were imported from Belgium, England, and France, mainly between 1880 and 1910. From 1910 to 1945 there were no outside crosses, but after World War II Anglo-Normans were used again and some Arab blood was introduced.

Normally bay or chestnut, the Freiberger stands 14.3 to 15.2 hands and weighs between 1,200 and 1,450 pounds. This compact and very active animal has a well-muscled body and strong, hard limbs and hoofs. The breed is employed in agriculture, especially in hilly areas, and it is also used by the army for draft, pack, and riding purposes in the mountains. Although the breeding stock shows a high degree of standardization, there is still sufficient variation between the different bloodlines to satisfy individual requirements for horses of a lighter or heavier stamp.

Friesian

A breed of ancient origin, the Friesian was used in the Middle Ages as a warhorse and later as a charger. It is native to the northern Dutch province of Friesland, an area of rich pasture ideal for producing horses of a heavy stamp. During the nineteenth century a stud book was opened, but the popularity of the Friesian declined to such an extent that by 1913 the number of registered stallions had been reduced to three. However, a society was formed to preserve the breed and its numbers have since steadily increased.

The modern Friesian is always black (a small white star on the face is the only marking allowed) and has a profuse mane and tail. It stands about 15 hands and has a neat head set on a shapely, upright neck; a round-ribbed body with a strong back and low-set tail; and hard, heavily feathered legs with open blue hoofs. A docile, yet active and willing worker, noted especially for its high action at the trot, the Friesian is used for farm work and in harness.

▲ Freiberger ▼ Friesian

Groningen

The Dutch Groningen, basically an offshoot of the German Oldenburg, was formerly a very popular draft breed. It was found not only in Groningen but also in Friesland, Drenthe, and a number of other provinces. However, because farming has now become a highly mechanized industry in the Netherlands, there has been a marked decline in the demand for horses of this type and breeders are now concentrating on producing riding horses. To this end Groningens are being crossed with Holstein, Tråkehner, and other stallions. As there are no longer any purebred Groningen stallions available, these crossings will eventually result in the disappearance of the original type.

Normally standing about 15.2 to 16 hands, the Groningen is black or brown, often with white markings on the face and legs. A docile, clean-legged animal, it has a refined head carried high on a longish neck and a deep body with a strong back, flat croup, and high-set tail.

124

Irish Draft

Although the precise origins of the Irish Draft horse are unknown, it has been suggested that it descended from warhorses and other horses imported into Ireland at various times.

The predominant colors are gray, bay, brown, and chestnut, and the height varies between about 15.1 and 16.2 hands. A quiet, docile creature, it has a good neck and head carriage, strong shoulders, and clean, extremely hard legs with plenty of bone. The Irish Draft horse is particularly noted for its free, easy, and true action and for its natural jumping ability. Because of its great stamina and ability to carry weight, it has long been favored for crossing with Thoroughbreds to produce quality hunters, show jumpers, and event horses.

In recent years there has been an increasing shortage of Irish Draft horses, but it is hoped that the bans imposed on the export of horses from the Republic of Ireland to the European continent for working purposes (1964) and slaughter (1965) will lead to a replenishment of home stocks.

North Swedish

The North Swedish horse is descended from a small, native Scandinavian breed, which, up to the formation of the breed society in about 1890, had been crossed with a variety of other breeds. From that time onward the only crosses were with the Døle, a closely related breed from Norway, and within about a decade a type had become fixed.

Bay, brown, chestnut, black, or, quite often, dun with black points, the North Swedish horse stands 15.1 to 15.3 hands. It is of medium build, with a deep, well-muscled body and strong legs with hard joints and hoofs. It has an exceptionally good temperament and is noted for its strength, longevity, sound constitution, and, above all, for its lively, energetic gaits. It is a particularly good trotter and is often raced in harness, especially in northern Sweden. It is also used in forestry and agriculture.

Dole

In its general appearance the Døle, or Gudbrandsdal, of Norway is very like the Dales pony of Britain; the two breeds are believed to have descended from common or very similar ancestral stock. The Døle has received infusions of outside blood of various kinds; the Thoroughbred stallion Odin, imported in 1834, is said to have had a particularly lasting influence on the breed.

Standing 14.3 to 15.2 hands, the Døle is black, bay, or brown, with a profuse mane and tail. It has a square head, a crested neck, strong, fairly long back, muscular shoulders and quarters, and short, very hard, feathered legs. A powerful, hardy, and very active animal—its best gait is the trot—it is used for haulage and in agriculture and forestry. The Døle is now being crossed with trotters to produce a lighter type of horse, suitable for riding and fast driving. **127**

Ardennes

Two quite distinct types of horse share the name Ardennes. The smaller, slighter, more lively type, standing about 14.2 to 15.1 hands, is now found almost exclusively in the area around Chaumont, in northern France. It is probably closer to the original ancient breed than the stockier, more familiar type, which is widely distributed through France and Belgium. This popular animal derives its extra height (it stands about 15.3 hands) and weight largely from Belgian blood. The influence of the Belgian Heavy Draft horse is particularly marked in the Belgian Ardennes and in its offshoot, the Swedish Ardennes (see p. 147).

The Ardennes is one of the most hardy of the heavy draft breeds. It is also noted for its docile temperament, its quick, vigorous action, and its great stamina—qualities that have made it ideal for farm work. Usually bay, roan, or chestnut, it has a deep, compact, heavily muscled body and short, very hard, lightly feathered legs.

Russian Heavy Draft

This breed is found mainly in the Ukraine, where it was developed about 100 years ago. Local draft mares were crossed with imported Ardennes, Percheron, and Orlov stallions, and the best of their progeny were interbred to produce a strong, hardy, but not overlarge horse, suitable for all kinds of agricultural work.

Not exceeding 15 hands (the average height is 14.2½ hands), Russian Heavy Draft horses are normally chestnut, dark chestnut, bay, or roan, with a full mane and tail. They have a massive, arched neck, a long, deep body with a broad back, short, powerful loins, and a sloping croup, and strong, relatively short legs with hard hoofs. These energetic, good-natured animals are noted for their remarkable pulling power and for their light, free action at the walk and trot.

Belgian Heavy Draft

In the Middle Ages Belgium was famous for its heavy horses. Flemish stallions played an important role in the development of a number of breeds, including the Shire and various French draft breeds. The Belgian Heavy Draft horse dates from the foundation in 1885 of the *Société Royale "Le Cheval de Trait Belge,"* which was responsible for eliminating inferior strains and establishing a uniform type throughout the country.

Thickset and stocky, the Belgian Heavy Draft horse has a relatively small, well-shaped head carried on a short, thick neck, a compact, well-muscled body with massive quarters, and strong, short, heavily feathered legs. Colors commonly found within the breed are sorrel, dun, red roan, and chestnut. In spite of its enormous size—it stands 16 to 17 hands and weighs over a ton—this horse is very mobile and active. Docile, willing, adaptable, and easy to handle, it matures early and is long-lived.

Boulonnais

Found in northwestern France, in the departments of Oise, Somme, and Pas-de-Calais, the Boulonnais is regarded as one of the most elegant of the heavy draft breeds. Although of different descent, it is remarkably like the Percheron and similarly has a considerable amount of eastern blood. This is thought to have been derived from Roman cavalry horses taken to France immediately before the invasion of Britain, in the first century A.D. and, later, from stock brought back from the Middle East by the French crusaders.

Usually gray, with a fine, silky coat, the Boulonnais has a small head set on a thick, arched neck, broad chest, straight back with short loins and powerful quarters, and clean, sturdy legs.

Since the seventeenth century two types have existed. The larger variety, standing up to 17 hands, is used for heavy haulage and in agriculture. The smaller type, now fast disappearing, is a lively, active animal formerly much used for pulling tradesmen's carts.

▲ Breton ▼ Clydesdale

Breton

Like many of the French draft breeds, the Breton, bred in northwestern Brittany, is represented by two principal types; both stand between 15 and 16 hands. The lighter variety, known as the Postier Breton, contains Norfolk Trotter blood introduced during the nineteenth century. Noted for its sound constitution and energetic action, it was formerly used extensively for work with light artillery and is now used mainly in agriculture.

The heavier type, the Breton Heavy Draft, has received infusions of Percheron and Boulonnais blood to increase its weight. It still does not rank among the "super heavies," but its combination of strength, hardiness, and activity have made the Breton a useful and adaptable farm horse. It has a broad head borne on a strong, arched neck, muscular, round-ribbed body with a double croup, and lightly feathered legs with plenty of bone. The predominant colors of the breed are chestnut, bay, and roan (red, strawberry, and, more rarely, blue).

Clydesdale

With the industrial expansion in Britain during the eighteenth century and the development of roads, shoulder haulage began to replace pack transport. In response to the consequent demand for heavier animals, farmers in the area of Scotland now known as Lanarkshire developed the Clydesdale, produced largely by selective mating within the local native breed but also by some crossing with Flemish stallions.

The Clydesdale stands about 17 hands and is bay, brown, black, or (more rarely) chestnut, with large areas of white on the face, legs, and sometimes also on the body. It has an open, straight-profiled head, a long, well-arched neck, and a close-coupled body with oblique shoulders and high withers. Breeders have always placed special emphasis on the feet, which should be hard, round, and open; and on the legs, which carry a good deal of feather and should be strong, straight, and planted well under the body.

For its size the Clydesdale is an exceptionally active animal, and this, together with its strength, stamina, and amenable disposition, have made it popular in many parts of the world.

Dutch Draft

One of the most massively built breeds in Europe, the Dutch Draft horse was developed in the Netherlands after World War I. The foundation stock consisted of native mares of the Zeeland type, which were crossed with imported heavy draft stallions from Belgium, including Ardennes.

Normally bay, chestnut, or gray, the Dutch Draft horse has a medium-sized head carried on a very short, thick neck. Its body is massive and deep, with heavy shoulders, a short, wide back, well-sprung ribs, broad, heavy quarters, sloping croup, and a low-set tail. The legs are well placed, strong, and muscular, and the feet are sound. Horses of this breed have a good action at all paces but are noted above all for their exceptionally quiet, willing disposition. Unfortunately, with the increasing mechanization of agriculture, Dutch Draft horses are no longer in such demand and their numbers are steadily declining.

Italian Heavy Draft

Based on the Breton of France, the Italian Heavy Draft horse is found throughout northern and central Italy. Standing 15 to 16 hands, this powerful horse may be dark liver-chestnut, sorrel, or roan. The medium-sized head is carried high on a short, powerful neck, and the body is well muscled and deep through the girth, with a short, dipped back and strong loins and quarters. The limbs are sturdy, with fairly small hoofs and a little feather at the heels.

Italian Heavy Draft horses are very docile and amenable, combining strength and stamina with exceptional speed and activity for their size. In spite of their eminent suitability for use in agriculture, horses of the breed are being produced increasingly for slaughter.

Jutland

The precise origins of this breed are uncertain, although a type of heavy warhorse is known to have existed in Denmark as long ago as the twelfth century. The best of the present-day Jutlands are said to have descended from Oppenheim LXII, a dark-chestnut Suffolk Punch or Shire stallion imported from England in 1862.

With an average height of about 15.3 hands, the Jutland weighs 1,500 to 1,800 pounds. It is commonly chestnut, often with white markings on the face and legs, although sorrels, roans, and other colors also occur within the breed. The head, of proportionate size, is carried on a fairly short neck. The body, which is broad, round-ribbed, long, and very deep, has a pronounced dip at the saddle, a long, sloping croup, and muscular loins and quarters. The sturdy, relatively short legs have some feather and the feet are large and rounded.

Jutlands are active yet very docile animals and were widely used in the past for agricultural work and heavy haulage; today their numbers are steadily decreasing.

Lithuanian Heavy Draft

The development of this breed, which is used for farm work and city transport, dates from about 1880. It was based on the native Zhmud. This small, hardy horse was crossed with various breeds, including (from about 1918) the Swedish Ardennes, to produce larger horses of a heavier stamp. The resultant crossbreds were used in a long program of selective breeding that resulted in the emergence of a fixed type, officially registered in 1963.

The Lithuanian Heavy Draft horse stands 15 to 15.3 hands and is commonly chestnut, although bays, sorrels, roans, blacks, and grays also occur. It is a strong, massively built animal, with a thick, arched neck, a long, deep, broad body, rounded, drooping croup, and short, powerful legs carrying some feather. There is also a finer, narrower, but taller type of horse of this breed, having a light head and a comparatively short body. Both standard and light types are calm and good-natured and have a good, free action at the walk and trot.

137

This page, Noriker; right, Muraköz

Noriker

The Noriker takes its name from the ancient Roman province of Noricum, in central Europe, where it was bred in Roman times. Also known as the South German Cold-Blood, it is now found throughout Austria and southern Germany.

Standing 16 to 16.2 hands, the Noriker is usually chestnut, bay, or brown. It has a heavy head with a straight or slightly convex profile, a short, thick neck, broad, deep chest, straight shoulders, and broad quarters with a low-set tail. Its legs are short and sturdy, with short, feathered pasterns and hard, flat hoofs. It has a long, sure action and is used mainly for haulage and farm work.

There are two regional sub-varieties of this breed: the Pinzgauer Noriker of Austria and the Oberlander of Bavaria.

Muraköz

Developed in Hungary and now bred also in Poland and Yugoslavia, the Muraköz is a relatively new breed, produced in the twentieth century. Native stock was improved by imported Percheron and Belgian Ardennes stallions to produce a strong, good-quality, fast, and active animal, which was in great demand, especially between the wars, for heavy agricultural work.

There are now two types of Muraköz: a heavier type, reaching a height of 16 hands or more; and a smaller, lighter variety. The predominant colors are chestnut, bay, and black, but occasional grays and roans are found. An economical feeder, the Muraköz is noted for its good constitution and docile temperament. It has a long head carried on a short, thick neck, a deep, close-coupled body with a sloping croup, and sturdy, lightly feathered legs.

Percheron

Strong, hardy, energetic, and easy to break and handle, the Percheron is one of the most popular and widely distributed of the heavy draft breeds. Its home is the Perche district of France, an area of rich pasture lying to the west and southwest of the Parisian basin, but the breed is also established in Britain, the United States, and Argentina, as well as in many parts of western Europe.

Gray or black in color, the Percheron stands 16 to 17 hands. It has a deep, compact body with sloping shoulders, a wide chest and strong back, and well-proportioned quarters. Its limbs are clean, short, and strong, with heavy, flat bone; its feet are hard and open, with bluish hoofs. The Percheron has a large proportion of Arab blood in its make-up, and this is particularly evident in its characteristically small, fine head, silky coat, and fine skin.

There is also a smaller, lighter type, known as the Percheron Postier, but its numbers are now declining.

Vladimir Heavy Draft

A strong, well-made animal standing at about 16 hands, the Vladimir Heavy Draft horse was developed in the Vladimir and Ivanovo regions of the Soviet Union, east of Moscow. Initially, local horses were crossed with heavy horses of various breeds, notably Clydesdales and Shires. The best of the crossbreds obtained in this phase were then mated with each other and a fixed type was gradually established.

The predominant color of the breed is bay, often with white markings on the face and legs. The Vladimir has a medium-sized head with a slightly convex profile, a short, thick neck, a long, fairly broad body, stout legs with a moderate amount of feather, and large, rounded feet. It is a willing, energetic worker, with a good action and a sound constitution.

Schleswig

Found in the extreme north of West Germany, this breed can be traced back to the Jutland of Denmark. Because the Schleswig was consistently maintained by the use of Danish stallions, a practice finally abandoned in 1938, the bloodlines of the two breeds are the same. In the nineteenth century the Schleswig was in great demand for pulling buses and streetcars. Breeding regulations were laid down in 1888, and in 1891 a stud book was opened, following the formation of the *Verband des Schleswigen Pferdezuchtverein*—a governing body still in existence today.

The Schleswig is a stocky, active animal with a quiet, willing disposition. It has a fairly large head set on a heavy, crested neck, a long body, sometimes with rather flat ribs, and sturdy, relatively short legs with some feather. The feet sometimes tend to be flat and soft. The average height is about 15.3 hands, and the predominant color of the breed is chestnut, although bays and grays are also found.

Shire

Said to have descended directly from the medieval warhorse known as the Great Horse, the Shire is the largest both in height and weight of the British heavy draft breeds. It is also reputedly the largest purebred horse in the world. An immensely strong, yet very docile animal, the Shire is still used in a few rural areas for agricultural work. In cities it has proved more economical than motor transport for short haulage, especially by breweries.

Black, bay, or gray, with characteristic white markings and heavy feather on the legs, the Shire has a medium-sized head, which is broad between the large, prominent eyes and is usually slightly Roman-nosed. Its neck is relatively long and slightly arched; its shoulders are deep and oblique, and its body is broad and muscular. The average height is about 17 hands, but stallions sometimes reach as much as 18 hands and weigh over a ton.

In Britain the principal breeding areas are Cambridgeshire, Huntingdonshire, and Lincolnshire. The breed is also established in a number of other countries, including the United States.

Soviet Heavy Draft

As a fixed breed, the Soviet Heavy Draft horse dates from about 1940. Its development began in the late nineteenth and early twentieth centuries, when, in a number of regions in the European part of the Soviet Union, Brabants, Ardennes, and Percherons were crossed with local horses. The best of the progeny were then used for selective breeding. Today the Soviet Heavy Draft horse is the most numerous and widely distributed of the heavy draft breeds in the Soviet Union.

Standing about 16 hands, it is usually bay, chestnut, or roan, with a full mane and tail and some feather on the legs. A good-tempered, active animal, with a large head, long body, and sturdy legs, it is used principally for farm work.

145

Suffolk Punch

As its name suggests, this heavy draft horse was originally from the English county of Suffolk. Although the breed is now found in many countries, including the United States, the descent of every living Suffolk Punch can be directly traced in the male line to a stallion called Crisp's Horse of Ufford, foaled in 1760.

About 16 hands and often weighing a ton or more, the Suffolk is invariably chestnut. It has long, muscular shoulders, a deep, powerful, round-ribbed body with a girth measurement of over 8 feet, and short, clean legs with up to 11 inches of bone. A docile, active animal with a hardy constitution, the Suffolk is noted for its longevity and its ability to exist on poor food. Although still employed for certain types of agricultural work, the breed is now used principally for short haulage, especially by breweries.

Swedish Ardennes

Based on Ardennes horses imported from Belgium during the nineteenth century, this breed was formerly much used in agriculture. Although increasing mechanization has led to a sharp reduction in its numbers, it still contains the largest proportion of Sweden's registered purebred stallions. Some Swedish Ardennes continue to be used on the more remote hill farms, but the majority are now employed in forestry for moving timber.

These very strong, active horses are noted for their equable disposition, hardiness, and longevity. They normally stand between 15.2 and 16 hands and weigh between 1,200 and 1,600 pounds. Compact and well built, they have a deep, muscular body, stout, hard limbs with some feather, and blue, open hoofs.

Glossary

amble: a two-beat lateral gait, similar to the pace but slower.

barrel: See diagram of horse (p. 152).

bay: having a dark-reddish to light yellowish-brown coat, a black mane and tail, and (normally) black markings on the limbs.

bay-brown: predominantly brown, with a bay muzzle and black limbs, mane, and tail.

bay roan: another term for **red roan.**

black: having a black skin, body color, mane, and tail, sometimes with white markings on the head and limbs.

blue: (of hoofs) dark blue-black: generally considered to be an indication of hardness.

blue dun: See **dun.**

blue roan: having a basically black or black-brown coat with an admixture of white hairs, giving a bluish tinge. The lower part of the limbs is usually black.

breed: a relatively homogeneous group of animals within a species that reproduces true to type. Breeds are usually produced by man, by selective mating.

brown: having a body coat consisting of a mixture of black and brown, a black mane and tail, and limbs that are black below the knee or hock.

cannon: See diagram of horse (p. 152).

canter: a slow gallop; a gait in three-time in which the hoofs touch the ground in the following sequence: near hind, near fore and off hind together, off fore; or off hind, off fore and near hind together, near fore.

chest: See diagram of horse (p. 152).

chestnut: having a bronze or copper-colored coat with a mane and tail either of the same color, a slightly lighter or darker color, or (more rarely) flaxen.

chestnut roan: another term for **strawberry roan.**

close-coupled: having a deep, compact body with well-sprung ribs.

cold-blood: designating any horse or breed of horse without Arabian or eastern blood in its breeding. In practice, since many so-called cold-blood breeds have been improved by the use of Arab blood, the distinction is based mainly on physical type: broadly, all heavy draft horses and most European native ponies are classed as cold-bloods. Compare **warm-blood.**

148 **color breed:** a breed registered according to color qualifications as opposed to breeding. Horses registered with a color breed are often also registered with another breed.

conformation: the structure and general physical make-up of a horse.

cow hocks: hocks that point inward when viewed from behind.

crest: See diagram of horse (p. 152).

croup: See diagram of horse (p. 152).

dished: concave in profile.

dun: 1. **blue dun:** having a black skin, mane and tail and a blue-black body coat, sometimes with a dorsal stripe and a withers stripe. 2. **yellow dun:** having a black skin and a yellowish coat, sometimes with a dorsal stripe, withers stripe, and bars on the legs.

ewe neck: a neck having a concave, as opposed to a convex, top line.

family: a group of related animals divided into a number of genera. The horse family, Equidae, today contains only one genus, *Equus*. In the past it contained many more genera, all of which are now extinct. Horsemen also use the term for the progeny of a particular breed sire.

forearm: See diagram of horse (p. 152).

forehand or **forequarters:** the head, neck, shoulders, withers, and forelegs of a horse, collectively.

forelock: See diagram of horse (p. 152).

gait: any of the different ways in which a horse moves by varying the rhythm, order, etc., of its foot movements. See **amble, canter, gallop, pace, rack, slow gait, trot, walk.**

gallop: a natural, fast, four-beat gait in which the hoofs touch the ground in the following sequence: near hind, off hind, near fore, off fore; or off hind, near hind, off fore, near fore.

genus (pl. **genera**): a group of related animals in the same family, divided into a number of species.

girth: the circumference of a horse's body measured immediately behind the withers. See also diagram (p. 152).

goose rump: a croup that falls away in an exaggerated slope from the highest point to the root of the tail.

gray: having a dark skin and a coat consisting of intermingled black and white hairs, often distributed in such a way as to form patterns. As gray horses age, the proportion of white hairs steadily increases, so that the coat becomes increasingly light and eventually pure white.

hand: a unit equal to four inches, used in giving the height of a horse; parts of a hand are expressed in inches. For example, 15.3½ hands is **149**

equal to 5 feet 3½ inches. The height is measured in a straight line from the highest point of the withers to the ground.

hindquarters: another term for **quarters.**

hock: See diagram of horse (p. 152).

hogged or **roached:** completely shaved off.

loins: See diagram of horse (p. 152).

mare: a female horse aged four years or over.

mealy: of the color of oatmeal.

muzzle: the lower part of a horse's head, including the nostrils, lips, and chin.

odd-colored: having a coat consisting of patches of more than two different colors.

open: (of hoofs) deep and wide at the heel, with a well-developed frog.

pace: 1. a two-beat gait in which the legs are moved in lateral pairs, i.e., near fore and near hind, off fore and off hind. 2. another word for **gait.**

pastern: See diagram of horse (p. 152).

piebald: having a coat consisting of clearly defined patches of black and white.

points: the muzzle, legs, mane, and tail: used in descriptions of the color of a horse.

pony: generally, a male or female horse not exceeding a height of 14.2 hands.

quarters or **hindquarters:** the part of a horse's body behind the barrel. See also diagram of horse (p. 152).

rack: a fast four-beat gait in which each foot is brought down singly in quick succession.

red roan or **bay roan:** having a basically bay or bay-brown coat with an admixture of white hairs, giving a reddish tinge.

roached: 1. (of the mane) completely shaved off. Also: **hogged.** 2. (of the tail) closely clipped at the top and thinned out below by pulling away some of the hair.

roan: having a coat that is basically black, bay, or chestnut, with an admixture of white hairs. See also **blue, red, strawberry roan.**

roman-nosed: having a head with a distinctly convex profile.

sickle hocks: hocks that have a sickle- or crescent-shaped contour when viewed from the side, so that the line from the point of the hock to the ground slopes forward as opposed to being vertical.

skewbald: having a coat consisting of clearly defined patches of white and of any other definite color except black.

slow gait: an artificial lateral gait that is similar to, but slower than, the pace and also smoother, because the legs do not move quite simultaneously.

sorrel: having a brownish-orange to light-brown coat.

species: a group of closely related animals of the same genus that interbreed to produce fertile offspring. For example, the genus *Equus* contains the species *E. caballus* (domesticated horse), *E. asinus* (domesticated ass), *E. burchelli* (common zebra), etc. Members of different species do not usually interbreed in nature but can be made to do so; their offspring are usually sterile.

stallion: an uncastrated male horse aged four years or over, especially one kept for breeding.

star: a small white mark on the forehead.

strain: a subdivision of a breed.

strawberry roan or **chestnut roan:** having a chestnut coat with an admixture of white hairs, giving a pinkish tinge.

trot: a natural two-beat gait in which the legs are moved in diagonal pairs, i.e., near fore and off hind, off fore and near hind.

walk: a natural, slow four-beat gait in which the hoofs touch the ground in the following sequence: near hind, near fore, off hind, off fore.

wall eye: an eye in which the iris, usually a pale, translucent blue owing to lack of pigment, is ringed with white.

warm-blood: designating any horse or breed of horse with Arabian or eastern blood in its breeding. In practice, the distinction is based mainly on physical type: broadly, all light saddle and harness horses are classed as warm-bloods.

well let-down: (of the hocks) long, low, and close to the ground, indicating that the cannon bone is short—a good point of conformation.

well ribbed-up: having flat front ribs and hooped back ribs.

well-sprung ribs: back ribs that are closely spaced and well arched.

white: having a white coat, mane, and tail. White horses may be Albinos (see p. 50), which are pure white from birth, or grays, which are dark at birth (see **gray**).

withers: See diagram of horse (p. 152).

yellow dun: See **dun.**

Anatomical Chart

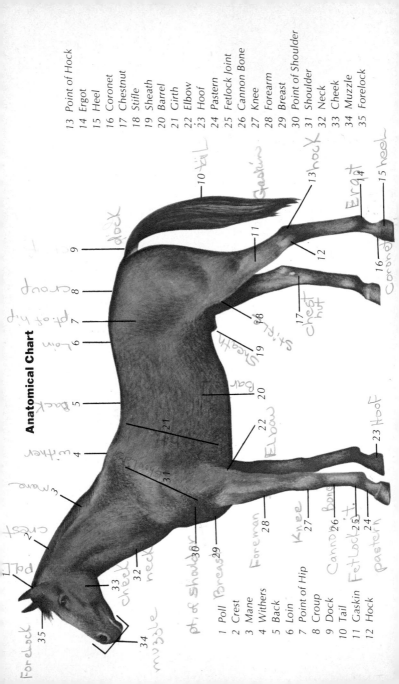

1 Poll
2 Crest
3 Mane
4 Withers
5 Back
6 Loin
7 Point of Hip
8 Croup
9 Dock
10 Tail
11 Gaskin
12 Hock

13 Point of Hock
14 Ergot
15 Heel
16 Coronet
17 Chestnut
18 Stifle
19 Sheath
20 Barrel
21 Girth
22 Elbow
23 Hoof
24 Pastern
25 Fetlock Joint
26 Cannon Bone
27 Knee
28 Forearm
29 Breast
30 Point of Shoulder
31 Shoulder
32 Neck
33 Cheek
34 Muzzle
35 Forelock

Horse and pony societies

Federation Equestre Internationale
Avenue Hamoir 38
1180 Brussels, Belgium

International Pony Breeders'
Association
Royal Dick Veterinary College
Edinburgh, Scotland

World Arabian Horse Organization
Woodpeckers, Nightingale Road
Ash, Aldershot
Hampshire, England

United States
American Albino Association, Inc.
P.O. Box 79
Crabtree, Oregon 97335

American Horse Shows Association
527 Madison Avenue
New York, New York 10022

American Saddle Horse Breeders
Association, Inc.
929 South Fourth Street
Louisville, Kentucky 40203

American Shetland Pony Club
P.O. Box 2339, Route 52 North
West Lafayette, Indiana 47906

Shetland Pony Identification
Bureau, Inc.
1108 Jackson Street
Omaha, Nebraska 68102

American Andalusian Association
P.O. Box 1290
Silver City, New Mexico 88061

Appaloosa Horse Club
P.O. Box 403
Moscow, Idaho 83843

National Appaloosa Pony, Inc.
112 East Eighth Street
P.O. Box 297
Rochester, Indiana 46975

Arabian Horse Club Registry
of America, Inc.
One Executive Park
7801 East Belleview Avenue
Englewood, Colorado 80110

International Arabian Horse
Association
224 East Olive Avenue
Burbank, California 91503

Half-Arab and Anglo-Arab
Registries
224 East Olive Avenue
Burbank, California 91503

Belgian Draft Horse Corp.
of America
P.O. Box 335
Wabash, Indiana 46992

Cleveland Bay Society of America
White Post, Virginia 22663

Clydesdale Breeders Association
of the U.S.
Route 1
Plymouth, Indiana 46863

American Connemara Pony Society
R.R. 2
Rochester, Illinois 62563

National Cutting Horse Association
P.O. Box 12155
Fort Worth, Texas 76116

Galiceño Horse Breeders
Association, Inc.
708 Peoples Bank Building
Tyler, Texas 75701

American Hackney Horse Society
527 Madison Avenue
New York, New York 10022

American Indian Horse
Registry, Inc.
P.O. Box 9192
Phoenix, Arizona 85020

The Jockey Club
300 Park Avenue
New York, New York 10022

Missouri Fox Trotting Horse
Association
Ava, Missouri 65608

Morgan Horse Club, Inc.
P.O. Box 2157
Bishop's Corner Branch
West Hartford, Connecticut 06117

American Mustang Association
P.O. Box 9243
Phoenix, Arizona 85020

National Mustang Association
Box 645
Cedar City, Utah 84720

Spanish Mustang Registry, Inc.
Box 26
Thompson Falls, Montana 59873

American Paint Horse Association
P.O. Box 12487
Fort Worth, Texas 76116

Pinto Horse Association
of America, Inc.
P.O. Box 3984
San Diego, California 92103

Palomino Horse Breeders
of America
P.O. Box 249
Mineral Wells, Texas 76067

National Palomino Breeders
Association, Inc.
East Dixie Street
London, Kentucky 40741

The Palomino Horse
Association, Inc.
Box 446
Chatsworth, California 91311

American Association of Owners
and Breeders of Peruvian
Paso Horses
P.O. Box 371
Calabasas, California 91302

American Paso Fino
Pleasure Horse Association Inc.
Arrott Building
401 Wood Street
Pittsburgh, Pennsylvania 15222

National Association of Paso Fino
Horses of Puerto Rico
P.O. Box 248
Carolina, Puerto Rico 00630

Percheron Horse Association
of America
Route 1
Belmont, Ohio 43718

Pony of the Americas Club, Inc.
1452 N. Federal
Box 1447
Mason City, Iowa 50401

American Quarter Pony
Association
Harold Wymore (Secretary)
New Sharon, Iowa 50207

Model Quarter Horse Association
P.O. Box 396
Lincoln, California 95648

National Quarter Horse
Registry, Inc.
Raywood, Texas 77582

Standard Quarter Horse
Association
4390 Fenton Street
Denver, Colorado 80212

Original Half Quarter Horse
Registry
Hubbard, Oregon 97032

American Shire Horse Association
300 E. Grover Street
Lynden, Washington 98264

American Suffolk Horse
Association
300 E. Grover Street
Lynden, Washington 98264

Tennessee Walking Horse
Breeders' and Exhibitors'
Assn. of America
P.O. Box 87
Lewisburg, Tennessee 37091

American Thoroughbred Breeders
and Owners Association
1736 Alexandria Drive
P.O. Box 4038
Lexington, Kentucky 40504

Thoroughbred Racing Association
of the U.S., Inc.
Suite 919
220 East 42nd Street
New York, New York 10017

The Trakehner Breed Association
Sankt Georg Farm
Rt. 1, Box 177
Petersburg, Va. 23803

National Trotting Pony
Association, Inc.
575 Broadway
Hanover, Pennsylvania 17331

United States Trotting Association
(Standardbreds)
750 Michigan Avenue
Columbus, Ohio 43215

U.S. Trotting Pony Association
P.O. Box 1250
Lafayette, Indiana 47902

Welsh Pony Society of America
1770 Lancaster Avenue
Paoli, Pennsylvania

EUROPE

Austria
Federation Equestre Nationale
D'Autriche
Haus des Sports
Prinz Eugenstrasse 12/111
A-1040 Vienna

Belgium
Federation Royale Belge des Sports
Equestres
Avenue Hamoir, 38
1180 Brussels

Denmark
Dansk Rideforbund
Vestre Paradisvej, 511
Holte 2840

Federal Republic of Germany
Deutsche Reiterliche Vereinigung
13, Lonsstrasse
D-4410 Warendorf/Westfalen

Finland
Suomen Ratsastajainliitto
Topeliuksenkatu 41a
00250 Helsinki 25

France
Federation Française des Sports
Equestres
Faubourg St-Honoré, 164
75008 Paris

German Democratic Republic
Deutscher Pferdesport Verband der
Deutschen Demokratischen
Republik
Nationale Reiterliche Vereinigung
Storkowerstrasse, 118
Berlin 1055

Great Britain
The British Equestrian Federation.
National Equestrian Centre
Kenilworth, Warwickshire
CV 82 LR

Greece
Association Hellenique
D'Athletisme Amateur
20, rue Amerikis
Athens (134)

Hungary
Federation Equestre Hongroise
Hold Utca, 1
Budapest V

Ireland
The National Equestrian Federation
of Ireland
Ball's Bridge (P.O. Box 121)
Dublin 4

Italy
Federazione Italiana Sport Equestri
Viale Tiziano, 70
Roma 00100

Netherlands
Nederlandsche Hippische
Sportbond
Waalsdorperlaan, 29a
(Postbus 117)
Wassenaar (Post den Haag)

Norway
Norges Rytterforbund
Postboks, 2401
Oslo 2

Poland
Polski Zwiazek Jezdziecki
Sienkiewicza, 12
Warsaw

Portugal
Federacao Equestre Portuguesa
rua do Arco do Cego, 20-5, 79
Lisbon 1

Spain
Federacion Hipica Espanola
Montesquinza, 8
Madrid 4

Sweden
Svenska Ridsportens
Centralforbund
Bragevägen 12,
114 24 Stockholm

Switzerland
Federation Suisse des Sports
Equestres
Blankweg 70
CH-3072 Ostermundigen

U.S.S.R.
Federation Equestre D'U.R.S.S.
Skaternyi Pereulok, 4
Moscow 69

Yugoslavia
Federation Equestre Yougoslave
27, rue Général Zdanov
Belgrade

SOUTH AMERICA

Argentina
Federacion Ecuestre Argentina
Rodriguez Pena, 1934
Buenos Aires

Brazil
Confederacao Brasileira de
Hipismo
rua Sete de Setembro, 81
Salas 301/2
Rio de Janeiro

MIDDLE EAST

Algeria
Federation Algerienne des Sports
Equestres
23, Bd Zirout Youcef
Algiers

Egypt
R.A.E. Federation Equestre
Egyptienne
Rue Kasr-el-Nil, 13
Cairo

Iran
The Iranian Equestrian Federation
c/o The Royal Horse Society
avenue Pasteur
Teheran

Morocco
Federation Royale Marocaine des
Sports Equestres
Polo du Souissi
Rabat

India
The Equestrian Federation of India
c/o R.V. Directorate
West Block III R. K. Puram
New Delhi 22

Australia
The Equestrian Federation of Australia
Royal Show Grounds, Epsom Road
Ascot Vale X 3032

Index

158

Kate Reddick has had a keen lifelong interest in horses and has written and edited several books on horsemanship. She lives near Newbury, Berkshire, in the heart of the English racing country, and is the owner of a part-Arab filly, from which she hopes to breed hunters.